THE MOSCOW & VORONEZH NOTEBOOKS

T0352418

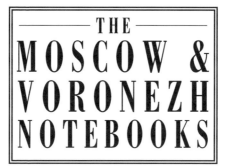

THE MOSCOW & VORONEZH NOTEBOOKS

Osip Mandelstam

POEMS 1930-1937

TRANSLATED BY
Richard & Elizabeth McKane

INTRODUCED BY
Victor Krivulin

BLOODAXE BOOKS

Copyright © Richard & Elizabeth McKane 1991, 1996, 2003

ISBN: 1 85224 631 6

This edition first published 2003 by
Bloodaxe Books Ltd,
Highgreen,
Tarset,
Northumberland NE48 1RP.

www.bloodaxebooks.com
For further information about Bloodaxe titles
please visit our website or write to
the above address for a catalogue.

Bloodaxe Books Ltd acknowledges
the financial assistance of
Arts Council England, North East.

ARTS COUNCIL ENGLAND

LEGAL NOTICE
All rights reserved. No part of this book may be
reproduced, stored in a retrieval system, or
transmitted in any form, or by any means, electronic,
mechanical, photocopying, recording or otherwise,
without prior written permission from Bloodaxe Books Ltd.

Requests to publish work from this book
must be sent to Bloodaxe Books Ltd.

Richard & Elizabeth McKane have asserted their rights under
Section 77 of the Copyright, Designs and Patents Act 1988
to be identified as the author of this translation.

This book brings together translations previously published
by Bloodaxe Books in two separate editions: *The Moscow
Notebooks* (1991) and *The Voronezh Notebooks* (1996).

Cover printing by J. Thomson Colour Printers Ltd, Glasgow.

Printed in Great Britain by
Cromwell Press Ltd, Trowbridge, Wiltshire.

For Peter Norman
and Sir Isaiah Berlin

ACKNOWLEDGEMENTS

For the translations of *The Moscow Notebooks*, we used the American edition of Osip Mandelstam's *Complete Works*, edited by G.P. Struve & B.A. Filipoff, 4 vols (Inter Language Literary Associates, 1967-81). The original Bloodaxe edition was the first to follow the order established for the Moscow Notebooks by Nadezhda Mandelstam (from the so-called 'Vatican Codex' copied out in Voronezh and committed to paper as well as to Nadezhda Mandelstam's memory). For *The Voronezh Notebooks* we used the Khudozhestvennaya Literatura two-volume edition of Osip Mandelstam, edited by P.M. Nerler with an introductory article by S.S. Averintsev and commentary by P.M. Nerler (Moscow, 1990). For the order of *The Voronezh Notebooks* we relied on Nadezhda Mandelstam's *Third Book* and Jennifer Baines's book *Mandelstam: The Later Poetry* (Cambridge University Press, 1976).

We are grateful to the publisher's reader Irina Kuzminsky for her very useful suggestions throughout the text of the *Voronezh Notebooks* poems. For the origin of many of the Notes, I am especially indebted to Pavel Nerler, and many members of the Mandelstam Society in Russia. Jennifer Baines through her book and in person gave support to the project, as did Sir Dimitri Obolensky who read Mandelstam with us at the Pushkin Club in London. The late Sir Isaiah Berlin, whose conversations with me about Akhmatova over 25 years were nothing short of inspirational, encouraged us generously and genially by letter and word. Victor Krivulin and Dmitri Vedenyapin made several valuable suggestions, and Peter Norman gave us support and inspiration.

This book's envoi by Nadezhda Mandelstam is her last letter to her husband Osip, taken from *Hope Abandoned*, first published in Great Britain by Collins and the Harvill Press in 1974, from the edition first published by Collins Harvill in 1989, copyright © Atheneum Publishers 1972, in the English translation by Max Hayward (Atheneum Publishers, New York, and Collins Harvill, London, 1973), reprinted by kind permission of the Harvill Press.

The poem titles in inverted commas are "contingency titles" either commonly used by the Mandelstams or created from first lines or from the poems by the translators.

RMcK

CONTENTS

The Moscow Notebooks (1930-1934)

SECOND MOSCOW NOTEBOOK

The Voronezh Notebooks (1935-1937)

The Moscow Notebooks

POEMS 1930-1934

Introduction

Osip Mandelstam was born into a Jewish family in Warsaw on 15 January 1891. The family moved to Pavlovsk, outside St Petersburg, very soon after Osip's birth. St Petersburg, Petrograd, Leningrad, or simply Peter, was to be *his* city. After his wanderings in the Crimea, Armenia, Georgia, and after living in Moscow, he returned there in 1930, and said: 'I've returned to my city of childhood illnesses and tears,/the city, that I know like the veins on the back of my hand.' (MN. I.9).

Petersburg was the city of Pushkin, Dostoyevsky and Alexander Blok, and of Mandelstam's contemporaries, the great poets Mayakovsky, Gumilyov and Akhmatova. In 1900 he went to school there at the privileged Tenishev Lycée, where he studied Classics, Humanities and Russian literature. He was already writing poems as a schoolboy. In *The Noise of Time* (1925), Mandelstam left an impressionistic portrait of the city – and his childhood.

In October 1907, having finished the Tenishev Lycée, he was sent abroad by his parents to Paris, returning to Petersburg in the summer. In November of 1909 he went to Switzerland and then on to Italy. As a young man he subsequently made other trips abroad. He was also a frequent visitor to Finland.

He attended Petersburg University from 1912 to 1917, but never graduated. In the spring of 1910 he went to lectures and readings of poetry at the Symbolist poet Vyacheslav Ivanov's 'Tower', the meeting place for many of the great Russian poets-to-be. It was partly from these gatherings that the Acmeist movement emerged, in which Anna Akhmatova, her husband Nikolai Gumilyov and Osip Mandelstam played the major roles.

As a young man, Mandelstam seems to have combined a savage shyness, with outspokenness, physical ungainliness and eccentricity. But when he read his poetry at readings in Vyacheslav Ivanov's Tower, or at the Stray Dog Café – the centre in Petersburg in the early 1910s of the century for performance poetry and cabaret – the audience was spellbound.

Mandelstam's first book *Stone* was published in 1913. *Tristia* followed in 1922. There then was a gap before a collection *Poems 1921-1925* was published together with *Stone* and *Tristia* in 1928, the year when much of his prose and critical prose was published. It was his last publication to appear in book form in his country for over thirty years.

His battle with time (he hated clocks, "development" and progress) and with his times, was resolved in the context of the Judaeo-Christian-Hellenic tradition. He valued that tradition along with the values of the intelligentsia and nineteenth-century Russian literature. Ultimately he believed that his poetry would transcend the times.

When he started writing the *Moscow Notebooks* in October 1930, he was actually in Tiflis, Georgia. He had not written any poetry for over five years. A scandal over Mandelstam's editing of two translations of Charles de Coster's novel *Thyl Ulenspiegel*, involving unjust accusations of plagiarism, had prompted his vitriolic, therapeutic *Fourth Prose*, written in Armenia. The Armenian trip, which lasted for eight months in 1930, liberated the Mandelstams from Moscow. It was only possible because Mandelstam had a powerful ally in the Kremlin, Nikolai Bukharin (who was later purged). Another factor that goaded Mandelstam to write poetry again was Mayakovsky's suicide in April 1930, which he heard about in Armenia, and a further spur was his friendship with the biologist B.S. Kuzin: 'I was awoken by friendship as if by a gunshot.' (MN. II.11).

The Mandelstams returned to Leningrad, via Moscow, in November 1930. They were only able to stay there for four months, since they were blocked by Tikhonov of the Writers Union: 'Mandelstam will not live in Leningrad. We will not give him a room' and 'Let him go to Moscow. Leningrad writers don't want him here.' Mandelstam was finally to get a flat in the Furmanov backstreet in Moscow, having led a vagabond life in Moscow and the south. This flat moved Osip Mandelstam to write one of the most horrific poems on life in Moscow (MN. II.17).

After the publication of the Armenian Cycle in *Novy Mir* and *Journey to Armenia* in 1931 in *Zvezda*, with its thinly veiled attack on tyranny in the closing passages (the editor was sacked), Mandelstam was not to be published again in his lifetime.

However, although Mandelstam was not published, he still gave readings. At one such reading in Leningrad in 1933, he was asked what he thought about contemporary Russian poetry. With his eyes flashing, he replied: 'What answer do you want from me? I am the friend of my friends! I am the contemporary of Akhmatova!' The crowd burst into applause.

When Mandelstam was ready he took on his 'equal', as referred to in the last line of 'The Wolf' (MN. I.15). In the winter of 1933 he read the 'Epigram to Stalin' (MN. II.20), to several people. It was the beginning of his confrontation with Stalin, for the poem reached the Kremlin through an informer. In a sense the epigram to Stalin was a more serious – and successful – suicide attempt than his jump from the window in the psychiatric hospital in Cherdyn, after he had been imprisoned in the Lubyanka and sent into exile. This proved, as some suicide attempts do, therapeutic: as he says in 'Stanzas': 'A jump and I am back in my mind.'

He began to write again in April 1935, and the marvellous *Voronezh Notebooks* followed, expressing a love of life and concern for humanity. It was at Voronezh that he wrote the untranslated 'Ode to Stalin', which is quite long, complex and far from adulatory. It was written down in a desperate attempt to save his wife and himself. At the end of his three year term of exile in Voronezh he lived briefly in Moscow, then Vaselovo and Kalinin, before his final arrest at a sanatorium in Samatikha on 1 May 1938. The Great Terror was at its height. Mandelstam was sentenced to five years' hard labour for counter-revolutionary activities. He died of 'heart failure' in a transit camp near Vladivostok in Eastern Siberia on 27 December 1938.

Nadezhda Mandelstam was his constant companion, his wife, helper, and his walking archive. It is due to her that his poems survive. In her books *Hope Against Hope* and *Hope Abandoned* she became the memoirist of her times, and the defender of faith of his poetry. Her determination, as well as Anna Akhmatova's, worked the miracle that continues through his poetry. Mandelstam has transcended the constraints of time and place which he so bitterly resisted. One hundred years after his birth, we can read, in English, his prophetic words: 'Yes, I am lying in the ground but my lips are moving.'

RICHARD McKANE
London, 1991

'The Moscow Notebooks': An Essay by Victor Krivulin

Moscow. Summer of 1917. A service of thanksgiving is in progress in the Uspensky Cathedral in the Kremlin: the patriarchate of All Russia, abolished by Peter the Great at the beginning of the 18th century, is being restored. The Petersburg period of Russian history had come to a close. At the same time, by a strange coincidence, the Petersburg period in the life of the poet Osip Mandelstam drew to a close. Motivated by a sharp historical intuition, Mandelstam suddenly left his native city and appeared in Moscow, where he discovered the old Russia of before Peter the Great, which was unknown to him as a European and a child of St Petersburg.

His first meeting with the old capital came about when he was in love with Marina Tsvetayeva, with a light and pure love. Later, Tsvetayeva was to write in her memoirs, how in the couise of those days she had 'made a gift of Moscow to Mandelstam'. Their walks together in the heart of ancient Muscovy, with its 'many-eyed cathedrals', were seen through the prism of the exalted admiration of the two poets for each other, though their own Moscow Golgotha lay in wait for both of them in the future. There were churches, full of people praying, the Asiatic, motley rows of stalls, and the stagnant silence of suburban blind alleys – all this seemed so unreal after swirling, revolutionary Petersburg.

But in the summer of 1917 forebodings as to what malevolent role the future Soviet 'whore Moscow' would play in the fate of the poet were drowned out by the sweet sound of bells which carried into Tsvetayeva's flat in the morning from the as yet undestroyed Church of Christ the Saviour. It seemed that the ancient city was living untouched by recent history, in blissful, prereflective ignorance of what was going on, in an atmosphere of Buddhist indifference to the increasing importance of the individual in the historical context. The paradox was that it was precisely this Buddhist Moscow which would itself turn in the 20s, into the centre of the new historic age, and into the symbol of a new epoch.

Mandelstam's first poems about Moscow, created at the end of the 1910s immerse us in a dreamlike reality of the present, penetrated by the past. The images of old Russian history find a meaning for the poet in precisely that historical moment when society as a whole, bewitched by the picture of the explosion of the revolution, spits on and tramples its own past in the name of the future. Mandelstam moves in opposition to the general flow and in the poems of 1917 turns to the most 'pitiful' episodes of Russian history, to the painful points of the nation's existence. So, in the poem 'On a straw laden sledge…' the complex chain of associations ties in the tragic fate of the murdered Tsarevich Dmitri and the heir, the Tsezarevich Alexey ('the whelp of Peter'), executed by his tyrant father, with the most recent victims of history. The poet foresees the possibility of these new victims so sharply, that the shooting of the tsar's family is seen as a natural and logical continuation, and the death of the poet himself is the finale, the full stop that ends the text.

At the end of the twenties, Osip Mandelstam and his wife Nadezhda settled in Moscow. The years of wandering round the Crimea, the Caucasus and the Ukraine were over. The poet did not want to return to Petersburg, which had lost its historical role as the capital of the empire. He chose the new spiritual centre of the new Russia. This was an attempt to accept the changes that were taking place, and to find an existential justification for them. It was a doomed attempt to find his own place in the new order of things.

Akhmatova was convinced that Mandelstam, by picking Moscow, had made a tragic mistake, which hastened his destruction. In Akhmatova's opinion, Nadezhda Yakovlevna, the wife of the poet, was partly responsible for this decision, since she couldn't accept his Petersburg friends and wasn't able to settle in his native city. But in the final analysis, this move was not simply about a choice of a different place to live, whether for psychological or material reasons – at the root of a matter was a radical spiritual reorientation and, even more, a doomed attempt to justify the advance of history.

Several contemporaries have left us with accounts which characterise the dominant mood of the Russian intelligentsia at the end of the twenties. Despite the fact that the regime was obviously getting crueller, those Russian intellectuals, who had been most vigorously anti-soviet and pro-western in the 20s, suddenly underwent a change of heart. The economic crisis in Europe and America somehow convinced them of the historical rightness of Bolshevism, and of the necessity not only of accepting the new order, but also of subordinating to it everything personal or 'subjective' ('the empty happiness of the few', in Pasternak's words).

Leningrad. December 1930. A last Petersburg cycle, completed after the Mandelstams' return to live in Moscow in January 1931, immediately precedes the Moscow Notebooks. It was here, in their first flat (if one doesn't count that of his parents') that his belated, hysterically desperate, but final, parting with his childhood occurred:

perhaps it was his way of settling of accounts with carefree infantilism – that eternal illness of the Russian intelligentsia, enchanted by rosy pictures of the wakening consciousness since the times of Leo Tolstoy.

No, it was with different memories that his Petersburg childhood returned of illnesses and hurts ('I've returned to my city of childhood illnesses and tears...' ['Leningrad', MN. I.9] about medicines ('cod liver oil of the street lamps on Leningrad's embankment'), of childish fears and phobias (oysters and guardsmen, in I.10). All this is recalled, of course, not without bitterness and regret that the torrent of time cannot be turned back, and always with a concentration on those dark, shadowy, detrimental aspects of what is first and foremost a highly intimate past, in order that it would be easier later to see the common, national-historic past as dark. He had to tear himself away from it, even if it cost him flesh and blood. For at the end of the twenties Mandelstam already realised clearly that to tear away his soul from the past was his only means of physical survival. The elemental attacks of 'Jewish terror', which were coming to life in the subconscious of the poet, not only forestalled, but also – and this can't be excluded – even provoked the intent stares of the 'un-sleeping eyes' of the police critics following him. He had not yet been accused of bourgeois cosmopolitanism ('Mandelstam is a poet of the *grande bourgeoisie*': that was how his position was defined in an article on him in the *Literary Encyclopaedia*) in the crisis year for Soviet culture of 1932 but he was already hastening to justify himself by exclaiming: 'I was a child in the world of the powerful...' [MN. I.10] and further on in the same poem, almost tuning in the keen ear of his future persecutors to the notes they needed, he denied the very things that he would be accused of later:

> I did not pose under the Egyptian portico of the bank,
> self-importantly in a fur hat,
> and the gypsy girl never ever danced for me, to the crackle
> of 100 rouble notes beside the lemon yellow Neva.

Such a Petersburg should be consigned as a fossil to the depths of the memory, and lie there corpselike, like a deadened 'winter of the soul'. The poet tries to save himself from its 'minor' childish fever, suicidally throwing himself into the embraces of the unembraceable all-Russian chill, beyond which he seemed to feel some inhuman warmth.

> so stuff me as you would stuff a hat into the sleeve
> of the hot fur coat of the Siberian wasteland.
> [MN. I.15]

14

Mandelstam felt that it was in Moscow that this inner national historical warmth was concentrated.

Moscow. Spring-summer 1931. The inner work on the reorientation of his conscience reaches a critical point. During these months Mandelstam attempted to carry through to the end a psychological operation on his past, on which depended not only his further existence in literature but also his very life. He did not succeed in this rescue attempt – fortunately for Russian poetry, but unfortunately for himself and those close to him.

Mandelstam returns in the Moscow Notebooks to the motif of 'the early times', although the subject matter is not so much childhood as a joint early 'season of life', where it is impossible to establish boundaries between boyhood, youth and student years. The best, purest and most festive things are subconsciously transferred from Petersburg onto Moscow soil, into another seemingly warmer and more favourable climate, into an atmosphere of spring and blossoming, of circus gaiety, music from booths, and simple enjoyment of the weather and seasons. The circus is presented as a joyful, risky, prototype of the youthful peoples' universe. (While I was reading Mandelstam's Moscow poems I kept remembering the 'circus' metaphors of Fellini's cinema, presumably because the childhood of the director coincided with the beginning of the thirties, and was spent in the tragico-farcical atmosphere of Fascist Italy, where the clown's booth (*8½* and *Amarcord*) travestied the mechanistic harmony of a new, totalitarian order.)

But here is Moscow in 1931:

> You'll say, 'Somewhere in the training square
> two clowns have settled in – Bim and Bom,'
> and the combs and little hammers start to play,
> now a harmonica is heard
> now a child playing
> a milky piano:
> Do-re-mi-fa
> and sol-fa-mi-re-do.
> [MN. I.25]

Intolerable scales, awkwardly played on an untuned *dacha* instrument, that tormented the ears and got on the nerves of most Russian literary figures – from Chekhov and Bunin, to Blok and Annensky, who inevitably touch on the *dacha* themes at the turn of the century. For them these sounds were inseparable from the suburban, Philistine, bourgeois way of life, whereas Mandelstam, reevaluating totally his attitude to the petty bourgeois (as his widow bears witness to in *Hope Against Hope* and *Hope Abandoned*), rehabilitating the 'little man' cursed by Gorky, refuses to qualify as vulgar this immature cacophony. On the contrary the motif of apprenticeship takes on an almost warring, military character in the Moscow Notebooks. It wasn't only the clowns, who, like the foot soldiers, settled in on the training ground to learn jokingly the Pythagorean-Leibnizian music of the spheres, but the poet himself feels that he is a soldier and thus calls up to his aid new moral teachers (the intellectuals of the 1860s, the battling nihilists and the spiritual bomb-throwers, who traced their genealogy from Herzen and the scholarly Vissarion Belinsky with his apotheosis of the plebs [the fourth estate]):

> Don't complain!
>   Is this why the intelligentsia
> were downtrodden so that I could betray them now?
> We shall die like the foot soldiers,
> but we won't glorify the looting, the hired labour, or the lies.
>   [MN. 1.25]

Here Mandelstam was retreating to positions he had prepared for himself at the close of the 1920s, when his relationship with the Russian intellectual, populist Narodnik-orientated literary party went through a radical change – from fastidious rejection of it, a rejection which was widespread among the modernists at the beginning of the century (see Mandelstam's article on Blok, 'The Badger Hole', where he rebukes the author of the long poem 'Retribution' precisely for its provincial, schoolboyish acceptance of the 'back to the soil' movement of the Narodniks), through a cautious anti-aristocratism in 'Conversation about Dante', to the hysterical but hopelessly belated 'wonderful oath of allegiance to the fourth estate' in the poems of the last Moscow period.

Why the enthusiasm for the role of student? Why does this intentionally democratic 'morning of life', with its boyish aggression, provide for Mandelstam the most serious moral alternative to the everyday Soviet hell? And is it really alternatives that he is searching for as he repeats with a rare insistence in various ways the verbs 'to teach' and 'to learn'; he, who at the outset of his writing career in the 1910s had polemically denied any form of enlightenment and teaching:

> There's no need to talk about anything,
> nothing should be taught,
> and the dark soul of the beast
> is so sad and good...

However it didn't turn out to be that good: witness not only the terrible experience of the revolution and of civilian chaos, but also

Mandelstam's own experience of growing old. What can withstand such experience? According to Mandelstam it turns out that it can be only 'discipleship', understood here as the highest form of the revelation of the self, and as a purposeful inner movement, but one directed from without. But discipleship is a state that pertains to youth and it is obviously 'not of his age or rank' for the aging poet. It was as though he was tempted to coax and coerce himself to feel young. Time and again in the Moscow poems there are imperative exclamations, calls on himself (the existential analogue of the slogan forms of political mass propaganda, which were widespread at the end of the twenties and in the early thirties) as though the poet were agitating himself, persuading himself ordering himself:

Get away! Don't ask for anything!

or

That's enough sulking.

or

Don't get excited: impatience is a luxury.

or

Guess why you've given Tyutchev a dragonfly...

or

(I) promise to build sturdy wooden frames...

or

Keep my words forever...

The great majority of these examples, in an analysis of verb forms in late Mandelstam, convincingly demonstrate an overwhelming preference for verbs used in the imperative, referring as a rule to the lyric hero himself. Thus, the schoolboy persuades himself to sit down to the hateful school books. The poet, if he wants to survive in the conditions of the "cultural revolution", must, whatever happens, feel that he is learning, is an apprentice, or at worst a student. To survive, for the poet, means to "re-learn" (that is to forget part of what he knows from before), and only after that to 'learn'. To learn, so as to become a 'teacher of the (new) life', so as to have the full moral right to declare about himself [a later poem from the Voronezh Notebooks – tr.]:

Yes, I am lying in the ground, but my lips are moving,
and what I say every schoolboy will learn:
the world is at its most curved on Red Square.

It is only with that consciousness of self that he can find a place worthy of him in the new society, which had passed at the end of the twenties from an infantile, pre-reflective, pre-revolutionary state to a state of juvenile aggression. In this society the teacher must feel that he himself is younger than his pupils, and indeed the concept of old age was taken as counter-revolutionary, and was subjected to moral and even legal discrimination, in the same way as, for instance, were the gentry or the merchant class. The young republic did not want to notice its old people, and if it did notice them, it was only didactically to juxtapose their powerlessness and conservatism with the living pyramids made up of young, trained bodies.

When it came down to it, during these years, the whole of old European culture was under suspicion – it had stopped being a social force, because it had proved itself incapable properly to secure the coming into being of the all-union festival of physical culture. But Mandelstam still lived on, thirsting to become young again, hoping for a 'second wind' which he should get any moment now 'on the race track', although he was now an old man, catastrophically balding (we should remember that even at the beginning of the twenties he had said in distress: 'A chill tickles my forehead / and I cannot admit immediately that time is cutting into me'). He was also suffering from asthma and heart disease, and, what was most dangerous in the circumstances, was bound by blood ties to the traditional European cultural values. (In that same year of 1931, Boris Pasternak discovered his second wind – he was able to adapt himself to the new conditions more successfully than Mandelstam.) However, Mandelstam's attempts to become young again were consciously doomed also for the reason that for the training ground where he tried out his endurance to find his youth anew, he chose the Faustian zone of European culture, or more accurately that creative 'longing for world culture', which he involuntarily associated with his own Acmeist youth. Unrestrainedly he filled the new Moscow poems to abundance not only with boats on ponds and rivers at holidaytime (that is the picture he creates of the park of 'Culture and Rest' on a Sunday, which used to be the Neskuchny Garden ['Neskuchny' means 'amusing' – tr.]) but also with heroic personages, transferred into the centre of the 'Soviet half-world' from the pages of school-books on the new European history of art – with Rembrandts and Mozarts, Raphaels, Titians and Schuberts.

Raphael goes to visit Rembrandt,
he and Mozart are in love with Moscow –
[MN. I.25]

His Moscow, in paroxysms of extreme rejuvenation, was already claiming the role of the eternally young world capital of the arts.

The poet endows it with everything which once fired his imagination: the Paris pneumatic post, the 'oozing Black sea jellyfish', the woven baskets for Asti Spumante; he takes telephone calls with Polish accents; he rushes, as though to the tap of an oxygen tent, to the fresh air of the museums, concert halls and galleries. (A parallel with Pasternak may be drawn appropriately here: in the book *Second Birth* ['Ballad' – tr.] Chopin, as played by Heinrich Neuhaus, thunders out triumphantly over the garages and parking lots, demonstrating the eclectic inculcation of the highest forms of world culture into the new industrial way of life. Pasternak is sensible: he stops on this note, not falling into an ethical apologetics of the old culture; for him the artistic past of man remains a one-way street, and the moral imperatives which classical art was guided by are only acceptable in part and with limitations.)

Unlike Pasternak, the lonely and unestablished Mandelstam runs the risk again of immersing himself entirely in mankind's golden dream of Renaissance: we should remember Blok's diary entry about the early poems of Mandelstam: 'They are like dreams, but dreams exclusively from the field of history of culture.' But now the poet turns to old European culture in order to, having found his spiritual roots in the splendid past, feel himself equally rooted in contemporary life, and to become a man 'of the epoch of the Moscow clothes Co-op', but without burying his hope for a new Renaissance.

The spiritual, aesthetic searchings of the poet get closer, however paradoxically, to the general direction of Soviet art, which had experienced in the thirties a half-enforced, half-voluntary reorientation – from avant-garde to Neoclassicism and Renaissance styles (the flowering of Palladianism in architecture). These tendencies were to appear more powerfully later in the post-war years but they were being formulated at the same time when Mandelstam, in his Moscow Notebooks, was painstakingly trying to correlate the aesthetic pathos of mass sport spectacles with the Renaissance cult of the human body. The Pre-Raphaelite 'young men in Verona (who) raced in the fields' [MN. II.6] and the Boccaccio 'youths, who once swaggered about in skimpy green undershirts' [MN. II.7] and Dante's 'athletic discoi' [from Mandelstam's later Voronezh Notebooks – tr.], strikingly remind one of the 'Italianate' depictions of Soviet sportsmen on the mosaic and *al fresco* panels, which decorated in abundance the halls of the first stations of the Moscow metro, the proletarian palaces and the houses of culture. The atmosphere of the first Moscow Notebook, reverberating with the morning and emphatically spring-like, corresponds with the general emotional atmosphere of the worst official art: there are the same key images and emblems: the morning, the flowering gardens, youth, the water festival on the background of the immense colonnade (of the Tuscan order) crowned with red and blue flags. ('The chattering light of the [Moscow] river crests / speaks of culture, rest and water' [MN. II.1]). It is enough to compare the popular Soviet song of those years, 'The cool morning meets us' with some of Mandelstam's lines, such as: 'It's getting light now. The gardens rustle with the green telegraph' [MN. I.25] and 'I am conscious that the beautiful year thirty-one is blooming in cherry blossom' [MN. I.26] to feel both the resemblance in emotional colouring and the fundamental difference: Mandelstam never pronounces 'we' in a pathetically social context. At best he reluctantly squeezes out of himself not simply 'I', but 'And I', shifting as the danger hanging over his head intensifies, to a forced 'But I' [from the later Voronezh Notebooks]:

> But, like a peasant who's worked his private land
> goes into the state farm, I go into life and the people are good.

This is the formula, this is the final limit of his attempt to accept Soviet life.

Well 'every schoolboy' knows now how voluntarily the peasant who's worked his private land went into the *kolkhoz*. The attempt to join expressed through 'And I' became not enough in the thirties for a legalised place in Soviet culture, and Pasternak, for instance, feverishly having searched for a moral formula of appeasement of the spiritual structure of his own personality with the victorious social order, settles on a distressed guiltily apologetic expression of his poetic personality: 'But can it be that I (am not measured by the 5 year plan?)' and he is in the role of, a naughty child subject to stern reprimands, periodic slatings, but never to have his head cut off. So to the end of his days he was to remain a student, never successful at ideology, abused, but never thrown out of the class, because his spiritual kindred (Shakespeare, Goethe, Schiller, all translated by Pasternak) continue to occupy, in the invisible Soviet literary hierarchy, unattainably high positions.

Osip Mandelstam did not take the road of an apologetic person with a civilising mission, not because he didn't want to, but because he couldn't. He couldn't, above all, because of aesthetic reasons. Andrei Sinyavsky once defined his own differences with Soviet authorities as 'aesthetic, not political', and this can be applied to the aesthetic rebellion of Mandelstam with much greater justification than to the ideologised prose of Abram Terts. The category of 'beauty' becomes for the poet an ethical and only *then* a political reference point.

In his one and only direct political invective against Stalin [MN. II.20] (the fact of its discovery breaks off the Mandelstams' Moscow period of life, abruptly changes his fate, throwing him into 'the external darkness' of the Cherdyn, Voronezh and Kalinin exiles) Mandelstam accuses the 'leader of the peoples' in the first instance on the basis of aesthetic criteria: Stalin is not so much terrifying as loathsome and repugnantly deformed: 'his thick fingers are like worms...' his 'cockroach moustache' bristles... The General Secretary is like a caricature of an operetta villain, and his moral degeneracy comes from there – he is the desecration of all the laws of beauty and goodness. The new way of life is deformed, the principle itself of the new power is anti-aesthetic ('power is as disgusting as the hands of a barber'). Nature is disgusting amidst which this power is being realised: 'The earth is seething with worms' [from a Mandelstam poem of 1921 – tr.]. Even the new Moscow is made disgusting, for the features of the leader appear there in portraits: this city where the decaying breath of the East can be clearly sensed, where 'the rings of boulevards swoon in black pock-marks' and 'the rain-moist worms are plumper', where the 'captive bear cavorts, the eternal opponent (Menshevik) of nature itself' [MN. I.25].

This city lives as though under the anaesthetic of a new art, which deprives life of breathing. 'Cinema for us is the most important of all the arts' (Lenin's words), and Mandelstam likens the Soviet cinemas to opium dens, where the very air of existence is poisoned.

> The crowds come out dead,
> as though they have been chloroformed
> from the continuously overcrowded cinema.
> [MN. I.25]

Even before the revolution Mandelstam had a guarded attitude to the cinema, although the 'sentimental fever' of the first silent reels did not seem to portend the power of the screen over the soul and consciousness of the masses as it would be utilised from the end of the twenties for the purposes of political manipulation. The cinema, by democratically putting all those sitting in the hall on one level, subordinated the spectators to an extra-human force [from a later Mandelstam poem from the Voronezh Notebooks]:

> Even silent fish have words now,
> and the talking picture coming off
> the wet sheet of the screen
> approaches me, you and everyone.

Moscow. July 1932. The first sound-film theatre opened. For Osip Mandelstam this fact meant something more than just another technical innovation. The young Soviet culture had found its own words, and no longer needed the teaching voice of the poet. A year earlier, in the summer of 1931, Mandelstam had perceived the new life as silent – without speech. He saw his spiritual task in becoming the voice, the larynx, the throat of the epoch: based on this was his attempt to accept the 'Buddhist', pagan, abandoned to the East-of-the-soul Moscow, Russia and Europe.

> What a summer! The young workmen's Tartar backs are glistening.
> Women's kerchieves are wound round their necks.
> They have narrow, mysterious shoulder-blades,
> and childish collar-bones. Greetings
> to the mighty pagan backbone,
> which will carry us through a couple of centuries.
> [MN. I.29]

The roar of loudspeakers, deforming the normal human voice, did not only deafen the crowds herded into the claustrophobic, enclosed spaces, but also the poet, who stopped being able to hear his own voice, finding only in convulsive suicidal attempts ('a jump – and I am back in my mind') a shortlived sensation of the real connection with the world of the powerful.

[1990]

Translated by Richard McKane

FIRST
MOSCOW
NOTEBOOK

1. 'This life is terrifying'

This life is terrifying for the two of us,
my comrade, with the generous mouth.

Our black market tobacco is crumbly,
and you sit cracking nuts, my simple little friend.

One could whistle through life like a starling,
or eat it like your nut cake.

But – both of us know it's impossible.

[October 1930]

2. Armenia

Work appears to the people here,
like a menacing six-winged bull.
And the early winter roses bloom,
swollen with venous blood.

I

Armenia, you cradle the rose of Hafiz,
and nurse your brood of wild children.
Your breathing is the breathing of rough peasant churches,
with their octagonal, bullish shoulders.

Coloured with hoarse ochre,
you lie far over the mountain,
while all that is here is a transfer,
soaked free in a saucer of water.

II

A lion created the colours
you wanted, Armenia,
with a half dozen
crayons snatched from a pencil-box.

You are a country of pedlars' fires
and pottery thrown from dead mud plains,
you survived the red-bearded Persian and Turkish *sardars*
hidden within your stones and clay.

Far from the tridents and anchors of Petersburg
where the withered mainland sleeps.
You saw all those who loved life:
the rulers who loved executions.

Here when the women walk
with the grace of a lioness
and the simplicity of a child's drawing
my blood does not stir.

How I love your malevolent language,
your young tombs, where the letters
are like blacksmith's tongs,
and each word is an iron clamp.

[21 October 1930]

III

I can see nothing and my hearing has gone now,
I'm left with only the colours of terracotta red and hoarse ochre.

For some reason I started dreaming of morning in Armenia,
I thought: let's see how the titmouse lives in Erevan,

how the baker bends over and plays blind man's buff with the bread,
how he draws out the moist skins of bread from the oven.

O Erevan, Erevan! Did a bird draw you
or a lion colour you with a child's crayons?

O Erevan, Erevan! Not a city but a roasted nut.
I love the careen of your babbling streets.

I have dog-eared my muddled life like a Mullah his Koran,
I have frozen my time and shed no hot blood.

O Erevan, Erevan, I need nothing else,
I don't want your frozen grapes.

[16 October 1930]

IV

As time dawned you stood at the frontier of the world,
holding octagonal honeycombs in your hands.
You covered your mouth – a damp rose –
as you swallowed your tears.

You turned away in shame and mourning
from the long-bearded Eastern towns
and now you lie on a couch in the pedlar's stall
they take the death mask from your face.

[25 October 1930]

V

Wind a handkerchief round your hand and plunge boldly
into the depth of the crown-bearing sweetbriar
till the celluloid thorns crackle.
We'll get the rose without scissors.
But be careful that the sweetbriar doesn't fall apart –
rose dust – muslin – Solomon's petal,
useless for making sherbet,
giving neither rose oil nor perfume.

VI

A nation of screaming stones –
Armenia, Armenia!
Calling hoarse mountains to arms –
Armenia, Armenia!

Eternally flying towards the silver trumpets of Asia –
Armenia, Armenia!
Generously distributing the Persian coins of the sun –
Armenia, Armenia!

VII

Although the powerful circular forest has been chopped down it's
    not in ruins.
Stumps, anchors of felled oaks of a wild and fabled Christianity.
There are scrolls of stone cloth on capitols, pillaged from a pagan store,
grapes the size of doves' eggs, the flourish of rams' horns
and crested eagles, with owls' wings, still undefiled by Byzantium.

VIII

The rose is frozen in the snow:
snow six feet deep at Sevan...
The mountain fisherman dragged out his painted sky-blue sled,
whiskered snouts of well-fed trout
are on police duty
on the limy lake bed.

In Erevan and Echmiadzin
the huge mountain has drunk the whole atmosphere,
one should charm it with an ocarina,

tame it with Pan pipes,
so the snow would melt in its mouth.

Snow, snow, snow on rice paper,
the mountain floats towards my lips.
I feel cold. I'm happy...

IX

The villager's horse stumbles,
clattering over the purple granite,
and scrambling on the barren foundation
of the resounding stone of the state.

The Kurdish children run breathlessly
after the horse, with bundles of cheese,
reconciling God and the devil,
giving half to each.

[24 October 1930]

X

The fibrous music of water
is luxury to the poor village.
What is this sound? Is it spinning a warning?
Keep away from me. Danger is imminent.

In the labyrinth of the misty refrain
an oppressive darkness gurgles,
as though a water sprite
had come to visit an underground watchmaker.

[24 October 1930]

XI

I shall never see you again
short-sighted Armenian sky.
I shall never again squint and look at
this nomad's tent of Ararat.
I shall never open again,
in this library of clay authors,
this beautiful land's hollow book
that taught the first people.

XII

Blue sky and clay, clay and blue sky,
What more do you want? Just squint
like a short-sighted Shah over a turquoise ring,
over this book of resounding clay, over the land of the book,
over the poisonous book, over the precious clay,
with which we torture ourselves, as with music and the word.

[Tiflis, 5 November 1930]

3. 'Don't tell anyone'

Don't tell anyone –
forget all you saw
the bird, the old woman, the prison,
and anything else.

Or as the day approaches
and you part your lips
the shallow shudder of pine needles
will overwhelm you.

And you will remember a wasp at the summer-house,
a child's ink-stained pencil-box,
or the blueberries in the forest
that you never picked.

[Tiflis, October 1930]

4. 'The barbed speech of the Ararat gorge'

The Armenian language is a wild cat.
It is the barbed speech of the Ararat gorge,
the predatory language of clay-baked cities,
the speech of hungering mudbricks.

The short-sighted sky of the Shah,
a turquoise blind from birth,
will never read the hollow book
of clay fired with black blood.

[Tiflis, October 1930]

5. 'How I love this people'

How I love this people living taut under strain,
sleeping, screaming, giving birth,
this people nailed to the earth,
who think each year is a century.

Everything you hear from across
the frontier sounds good;
jaundice, jaundice, jaundice,
in the cursed, mustard undergrowth.

[Tiflis, October 1930]

6. 'The people howl like beasts'

The people howl like beasts,
and the beasts are sly like people.
The wonderful official who was travelling without money or papers,
was sent to do hard labour,
and he drank the Black Sea wine
in the reeking tavern on the road to Erzurum.

[Tiflis, November 1930]

7. 'The Armenian language is a wild cat'

The Armenian language is a wild cat,
that tortures me and scratches my ear.
If only I could lie on a broken-backed bed,
consumed by fever and the evil plague.

Spiders fall from the ceiling,
flies crawl over the sticky sheets.
Squadrons of long-legged birds are marching
across the yellow plain.

The official's face is terrifying as a gun –
there is no one more pitiful, more ridiculous –
despatched on a mission, shunted off
with no money or papers into the Armenian wasteland.

'Go to Hell,' they say,
to the old postmaster who stole the money,
the former guardsman who wipes the spit off his face.
'Get lost, and don't ever come back.'

A familiar hello thunders at the door,
'Is it you, old chap? What an insult!'
Shall we go on collecting deaths
as the village girl collects mushrooms?

We were individuals and became the faceless mass,
What is our fate to be? – who gave the orders? –
it is the fatal thudding in our chests,
and a bunch of Erzurum grapes.

[Tiflis, November 1930]

8. 'On watermarked police stationery'

On watermarked police stationery
the stars are alive.
The night has swallowed up the spiny sticklebacks.
The little office birds write their RAPP reports.

They like to sparkle so much –
all they have to do is put in an application –
and permission is always renewed
for twinkling, writing and decay.

[Tiflis, October 1930]

9. Leningrad

I've returned to my city of childhood illnesses and tears,
the city that I know like the veins on the back of my hand.

You've returned to it. Open wide, swallow quickly,
the cod liver oil of the street lamps on Leningrad's embankment.

Begin to know again December's short day,
when egg yolk is mixed with malevolent pitch.

I do not want to die yet, Petersburg! You still have
all my friends' telephone numbers.

Petersburg! I still have the addresses
from which I can find the voices of the dead.

I live up a back flight of stairs, and when they tear at the bell pull
the ringing hits me in the head.

I wait until dawn for the dear guests to arrive,
and each rattle of the slender door chain is like the clank of shackles.

[Leningrad, December 1930]

10. 'I was a child in the world of the powerful'

I was a child in the world of the powerful.
I was frightened of oysters and looked at guardsmen distrustfully.
I am not bound to it by even the tiniest fragment of my soul
no matter how much I once tormented myself to be part of it.

I did not pose under the Egyptian portico of the bank,
self-importantly in a fur hat,
and the gypsy girl never ever danced for me, to the crackle
of 100 rouble notes beside the lemon yellow Neva.

I took so much embarrassment, stress and grief
from the tender Europeanised beauties of my past,
and sensing future executions I escaped from the roar of revolution
to the Nereids by the Black Sea.

So why does this city have the right
to dominate my thoughts and feelings to this day?
Fires and frost have made it even more brazen,
arrogant, cursed, empty and youthful.

Is it because I once saw a children's picture
of Lady Godiva with her red mane of hair?
I still whisper to myself again and again:
'Farewell Lady Godiva, Godiva, it's all over...'

[January 1931]

11. 'Let's sit in the kitchen together'

Let's sit in the kitchen together,
smelling the sweet kerosene.

There is a sharp knife and a loaf of bread –
you could pump up the fuel stove,

or find some bits of string
to tie up the bundle before dawn,

so that we can go to the station
where no one can find us.

[January 1931]

12. 'Help me, O Lord, to live through this night'

Help me, O Lord, to live through this night.
I fear for life, for Your handmaiden.
Living in Petersburg is like sleeping in the grave.

[January 1931]

13. 'After midnight the heart steals'

After midnight the heart steals
forbidden silence from the hands.
It lives quietly, but is mischievous,
loves me, loves me not – it's not like anything else.

Loves me, loves me not, it understands, but can't catch me.
Why then does it tremble like an abandoned baby?
Why does the heart feast at midnight,
having taken a bite out of a silvery mouse?

[Moscow, March 1931]

14. 'Sherry brandy'

Ma voix aigre et fausse

I tell you absolutely
straight:
it's sheer raving and sherry brandy,
my angel.

There where Greeks saw
beauty,
squalor gaped at me from
black holes.

The Greeks took Helen
off across the sea,
but for me it's only bitter salt
on the lips.

Emptiness slaps me
in the mouth.
Poverty shoves me and says:
'Bugger off!'

Go on, do what you like,
who cares.
Angel Mary, drink your wine,
and never stop.

I'll tell you absolutely
straight:
it's sheer raving and sherry brandy,
my angel.

[Zoological Museum, Moscow, March 1931]

15. 'The Wolf'

I have forsaken my place at the feast of my fathers
and lost my happiness and even honour,
in order that future centuries may thunder with glory,
and that humanity may be noble.

This age of the wolfhound hurls itself on my shoulders,
but my blood's not the blood of a wolf,
so stuff me as you would stuff a hat into the sleeve
of the hot fur coat of the Siberian wasteland:

so I won't see the débris or the slushy mud,
or the bloodied bones strapped to the wheel,
so all through the night the blue polar foxes
will shine at me in their primeval beauty.

Take me off into the night where the Yenisey flows
and the pine tree reaches the stars;
my blood is not the blood of a wolf –
only an equal will kill me.

[17-28 March 1931]

16. 'It is night outside'

It is night outside. The deceit of the rich is all around.
It's 'après moi le déluge'.
And then what? The citizens will be hoarse,
and there'll be a crowd in the cloakroom.

Masked ball, wolfhound age.
Learn by heart the lesson:
stuff your hat up your sleeve,
and may God preserve you!

[March 1931]

17. 'Alexander Herzowitz'

Once upon a time there lived
a Jewish musician named Alexander Herzowitz.
He polished his Schubert
as if it were a sparkling jewel.

From morning till evening
he played incessantly
one eternal sonata
that he'd learned by heart.

Isn't it dark outside
Alexander Herzowitz?
Give it up Alexander Scherzowitz,
what's the use?

Let the Italian girl
fly after Schubert
on a narrow sledge
across the crunching snow.

We're not afraid to die
with the dove music,
and then to hang like a black
coat on the hook.

Alexander Heartsowitz,
it's all been played before.
Give it up Alexander Scherzowitz,
what's the use?

[27 March 1931]

18. 'Eyelashes sting with tears'

Eyelashes sting with tears as a sob wells up in the chest.
I sense the storm is imminent but I am not afraid.
Someone wonderful hurries me to forget something,
I feel I'm being smothered yet I want to live to the point of dying.

At the first sound I rise from the bunks,
looking around me with wild and sleepy eyes,
thus a prisoner in a rough coat sings a convict song
as the strip of dawn rises over the labour camp.

[March 1931]

19. 'I can't hide from the chaos'

I can't hide from the chaos
behind the Moscow cab driver's back –
I'm hanging on the tram strap of these terrible times,
and I don't know why I'm alive.

Let's take route A or route B
to see which one of us will die first.
The city huddles like a sparrow,
or rises like an airy cake,

and scarcely has time to threaten us from the street corners.
You do what you like, but I won't take risks.
Not all of us have gloves that are warm enough
to enable us to travel over the curves of whore Moscow.

[April 1931]

20. Untruth

With a smoking torch I go into
the hut to the six-toed untruth.
'Well, come on then, let me look at you.'
After all I too will have to lie in a pine coffin.

And she takes a pot of pickled mushrooms
out from under the bunks,
and gives me a piping-hot stew
of babies' umbilical cords.

'If I want,' she says, 'I'll give you some more,'
and I hardly dare breathe, and feel sick.
I rush to the door, but it's no good.
She grabs me and drags me back.

There are lice, moss and silence in the bedroom
jail of her remote hut.
'It's all right, you're fine...
I'm the same as you, old girl.'

[4 April 1931]

21. 'I drink to the military asters'

I drink to the military asters, to all that they blamed me for,
to aristocratic furs, to asthma, and to the spleen of the Petersburg day,

to the music of Haute Savoie pines, gasoline fumes on the Champs
    Elysées,
to roses inside a Rolls-Royce, to Parisian oil paintings.

I drink to the waves of the Bay of Biscay, to jugs of Alpine cream,
to the ginger arrogance of English women, and quinine water in
    distant colonies.

I raise a toast – but I still haven't decided which wine to drink –
the gay Asti Spumante or the sombre Château Neuf du Papes.

[11 April 1931]

22. The Grand Piano

The huge hall can scarcely breathe,
like the French revolutionary parliament deciding the fate of the
    opposition.
The bourgeoisie do not fight in the Gironde,
society is torn apart.

The shameful Goliath grand piano
is shamed by the discord
the lover of sounds, the mover of souls is
turned into a demagogue haranguing the crowd.

Master Henrik hops as if he were on a hobby horse,
his tail coat flapping.
Are my hands sledgehammers?
My ten fingers a little herd of horses!

If the world is to be made broader
and consequently more complex,
don't smear the keyboard
with a sweet potato.

There is a Nuremberg spring
which straightens out dead bones,
so that the gin-soaked sonata
should ooze like pitch from the vertebrae.

[16 April 1931]

23. 'Keep my words forever'

Keep my words forever, because of their aftertaste of sadness and
     smoke,
their resin of circling patience, and because my conscience laid the
     molten tar of work.
The water in ancient Russian wells must be black and sweet to the
     taste,
so that by Christmas the star would be reflected in it with all its seven
     fins.

In return for this, my father, my friend and coarse helper,
I, the unacknowledged brother, a splinter from the family tree,
promise to build sturdy wooden frames
for wells in which the Tartars will submerge the Russian princes.

If only these chilling executioner's blocks loved me!
Sticks are being thrown in the garden in a deadly game.
So for this I will wear a shirt of iron all my life,
and I shall find an axe in the forest for the beheadings beloved of
  the Tsar.

[3 May 1931]

24. Canzone

Tomorrow will I really see
the hoarders of the mountain landscape,
the monopolists of granite?
The heart beats with glory.

The eagle-eyed professors,
Egyptologists and numismatists,
are sombre-crested birds
with their tough flesh and broad breasts.

Now Zeus with the golden fingers
of a cabinet-maker twiddles
the remarkable onion lenses,
the gift of the Psalmist to the seer.

He looks through the exquisite binoculars of Zeiss,
the expensive present from King David,
and sees all the wrinkles in the granite,
and a pine tree or a village as small as an insect.

I'll forsake the land of the Hyperboreans
to feast my eyes on the last act of fate.
I'll say 'This is for ever' to the Rabbi elder
for his crimson embrace.

The edge of unshaven mountains cannot be seen yet,
the scrub growth is prickly,
and, like a newly-washed fable,
the green valley is fresh and bitter.

I love the army binoculars
with their usurous magnification of vision.
The world has only two unfaded colours left:
the yellow of jealousy and the red of impatience.

[26 May 1931]

25. Midnight in Moscow

It is midnight in Moscow. The Buddhist summer is luxurious.
The streets disperse in a shallow staccato of pointed ironshod boots.
The rings of boulevards swoon in black pock-marks.
It's not calm in Moscow even at night,
as peace runs from under horses' hooves.
You'll say, 'Somewhere in the training square
two clowns have settled in – Bim and Bom,'
and the combs and little hammers start to play,
now a harmonica is heard
now a child playing
a milky piano:
Do-re-mi-fa
and sol-fa-mi-re-do.

There were times, when I was younger,
that I'd go out in a rubber mackintosh glued together,
into the broad splayed-out paws of the boulevards
where the gypsy's skinny ankles beat against her hem,
where the captive bear cavorts,
the eternal opponent of nature itself.
The scent of the cherry-laurel was overbearing.
Where are you going? There are no laurels or cherries...

I shall tighten the weight
of the fast running kitchen clock.
My God, this time is rough,
and yet I love to catch it by the tail.
It's not to blame for its own pace,
and yet it is a petty thief.

Get away! Don't ask for anything!
Don't complain!
                 Is this why the intelligentsia
were downtrodden so that I could betray them now?
We shall die like footsoldiers,
but we won't glorify the looting, the hired labour, or the lies.

When I die you will cover me
with our threadbare tartan blanket as if with a flag.
Let's drink, my little friend,
to the oatmeal dregs of our sad fate.

The crowds come out dead
as though they have been chloroformed
from the continuously overcrowded cinema.
How venous they are
and how much they need oxygen!

It's about time you knew, I too am a man of my time.
I live in the age of the Moscow Clothes Co-op.
Look how badly my jacket fits;
how I walk and talk.
If you tried to tear me from the age,
I swear you'd break your neck.

I talk with the epoch,
but does it really have the soul of a demagogue?
Has it lived off us as shamefully
as a wrinkled little beast in a Tibetan temple?
It scratches and is put in a tin bath.
'Let's have another drink, monkey.'

Although it is insulting you should know that
there is fornication in work, and it is in our blood.

It's getting light now. The gardens rustle with the green telegraph.
Raphael goes to visit Rembrandt,
he and Mozart are in love with Moscow –
for its hazel eyes, for the drunken banter of its sparrows.
The draughts are passed from flat to flat
as if on an aerial conveyor belt,
like the ooze of the Black Sea jellyfish,
or the pneumatic postal service,
like the hooligan students in May.

[May – 4 June 1931]

26. 'That's enough sulking'

That's enough sulking. Shove the papers in the desk drawer.
I am seized by a glorious devil,
as if the roots of my scalp
had been shampooed by François, in the Paris of my youth.

I'll bet that I'm not dead yet,
and, like a jockey, I'll stake my neck
that I can still play tricks
on the race track.

I am conscious that the beautiful year
thirty-one is blooming in cherry blossom,
that the rain-moist earthworms are plumper,
and all of Moscow is going sailing.

Don't get excited, impatience is a luxury.
I will gradually increase my speed,
Let's go out onto the track at a cool pace.
I have kept my distance.

[7 June 1931]

27. Fragments from Destroyed Poems

I

In the thirty-first year from the birth of the century
I returned, no, was forced
to return to Buddhist Moscow,
but before then I saw
rich Ararat with its Biblical tablecloth
and spent two hundred days in the Sabbath land
which is called Armenia.

If you want a drink, there is good water
from the Kurdish mineral spring Arzni.
the most honest water, sharp and metallic.

II

Now I love the Moscow laws,
now I don't long for the Arzni water –
in Moscow there's the laurel-cherry and the telephones
and the days are distinguished by executions.

III

When you feel you want to live, then smile
at the milk tinged with Buddhist blue,
and look at the Turkish drum,
as it rushes back from
a public funeral on a red hearse.
You will meet a cart carrying cushions,
and you will say 'Go home geese and swans!'

Don't focus, just click dear Kodak,
the eye is a lens in a bird at a banquet
and not a piece of glass. More light and shade!
More! More!
The retina is hungry...

IV

I am no longer a child.
                        You, grave,
don't dare to teach the hunchback. Be quiet!
I speak for everyone, and with such power,
so that the palate of the mouth would become the vault of the sky,
and the lips crack like pink clay.

[6 June 1931]

V

The tongue-bear lumbers clumsily
in the cave of the mouth. And from Psalmist
to Lenin: so that the palate of the mouth would become the vault
        of the sky,
so that the lips would crack like pink clay,
more, more...

28. The Horse-cart Driver

On a high mountain pass
in the Moslem district
we sat down to feast with death,
knowing a fear we had only felt in dreams.

From nowhere appeared a horse-cart driver,
whose face was burned and wrinkled as a currant,
He was monosyllabic and sullen
like the devil's hired hand.

Then he grunted out 'cart' in Azerbaijani,
and clicked his tongue to get his horses going,
while he guarded his face from us
jealously, as if it were a rose or a toad.

Hiding his terrible features
behind a leather mask,
he whipped his horses,
off to somewhere, until their last gasp.

We were shoved back and forth
and couldn't get down the mountainside.
Horse carts flashed past,
wayside inns flashed past.

I came to with a jolt. 'Hey, friend, stop!'
Damn it, now I remember:
he is the Minister of the Black Death,
with his horses gone astray.

His disfigured destiny
drives us to the delight of his soul,
so that the bitter-sweet earth
could whirl endlessly like a merry-go-round.

There in Nagorno Karabakh,
in the predatory town Shusha
I experienced this terror,
which was born into my soul.

Forty thousand dead windows
look out at us from all sides
and the soulless shell of lives' work
is buried on the mountains.

The houses stripped shamelessly
stand pink in their nakedness,
and the blue-black plague of the sky
is barely visible.

                    *   *   *

Tender calves
and frisky playful steers,
and like ships in ranks,
she buffaloes with male buffaloes,
and finally the priestly bulls.

Like a crowd of people
massing forward, causing the earth to burst
into sweat, the layered herd of cattle
sailed directly at us
like an armada in the dust.

[June 1931]

29. 'After having dipped one's little finger'

After having dipped one's little finger
in the Moscow river one can now
peel the transfer off the Robber Kremlin.
These pistachio green dovecotes are so beautiful
that one should scatter them millet or oats.
The Ivan the Great belltower
is a huge adolescent dunce, despite its age.
It should be sent abroad to finish
its education. But what's the use? It's a disgrace.

The whole town lies open before us:
the suburban gardens and the factories
whose four chimneys shroud the water with smoke
seem to be bathing in the Moscow river.
Having thrown back the rosewood top
of the thundering grand piano
that is Moscow, we will probe
into its sonorous insides.
White guardsmen haven't you seen or heard it?

It seems to me that our time, like any other time,
is illegal. As a young boy follows the grown-ups
into the wrinkled waters,
I will go into the future
and, it seems, I will not see it.

I'll never walk in step with the lads
into the regimented sports arenas.
I won't jump from my bed at dawn,
woken by the dispatch rider with my call-up papers,
and I will not, even as a shadow,
enter the nightmarish crystal palaces.

Every day I find it more difficult to breathe,
but meanwhile I cannot gamble for time.
Only the heart of man and horse
are born to enjoy the race.

Faust's banal and youthful devil
leaps on the old man's ribcage,
and suggests I go boating for an hour,
or walking on the Sparrow Hills
or whip round the city on a tram.
Moscow's busy. Today she's nanny,
fussing over her forty thousand charges in their cradles.
She's alone, spinning the thread of destiny.

                    *   *   *

What a summer! The young workmen's Tartar backs are glistening.
Women's kerchieves are wound round their necks.
They have narrow, mysterious shoulder-blades,
and childish collar-bones. Greetings
to the mighty pagan backbone,
which will carry us through a couple of centuries.

[July – August 1931]

30. 'I've many years to live'

I've many years to live before I'm a patriarch.
I'm at an age that commands little respect.
They swear at me, behind my back,
in the senseless, pointless language of tram fights.
'You bastard!' Well, I apologise,
but deep down I don't change at all.

When you think of your connection with the world
you can't believe it. It is nonsense.
A midnight key from someone else's flat,
a silver penny in the pocket,
and stolen film.

I hurl myself like a puppy at the hysterical
ringing of the telephone.
I hear greetings spoken in Polish,
a gentle long distance rebuke,
or an unfulfilled promise.

You're always thinking about what you really desire
in the midst of all the crackers and fireworks.
Then you burst, and all that's left
is confusion and being out of work.
Just try even getting a light for a cigarette from that.

I smile at times, at times I timidly dress up
and go out with my white-knobbed cane.
I listen to sonatas in the backstreets.
My mouth waters as I pass by food-stalls.
I leaf through books in muddy doorways,
and I'm not living but somehow I am.

I shall walk to the sparrows and the reporters
and the street photographers who will take my picture,
and in five minutes pull it out
like a wet spade from a child's bucket,
and I'll look at my likeness
against the backdrop of the purple Shah mountain.

Or I'll go on errands
into the steamy basement laundry
where the clean, honest Chinamen
eat fried dough balls with chopsticks
and play with narrow cut cards,
and drink vodka as the swallows sip the Yangtse.

I enter the robbers' paradise of museums
where Rembrandt paintings gleam
like rubbed Cordoba leather.
I'll gaze at the Titian priests in tricorn hats,
and wonder at Tintoretto's thousand squawking parrots.

And how much I want to be carried away by play,
to have a conversation, to speak the truth,
to blow my depression to the mist, the devil and to hell,
to take someone by the hand and say to him 'Be kind –
we're on the same road.'

[21 August – 19 October 1931]

SECOND
MOSCOW
NOTEBOOK

1. 'The factories, bathing in the Moscow river'

The factories, bathing in the Moscow river,
spin cotton; and the broad green gardens stretch alongside it.
The chattering light of the river crests
speaks of culture, rest and water.

The tubercular, foppish, bureaucratic river,
the Lenin hills, above the Neskuchny Gardens which are the boring
        consistency of halva,
are the stamps and postcards, which like ships
carry us now and into the future.

The Oka river has raised an eyebrow,
that's why there's a breeze on the Moscow river.
Her little sister Klyazma's eyelashes flutter,
that's why the ducks swim on the Yauza.

The Moscow river smells like post-office glue,
the bell-mouthed loudspeakers blare out Schubert.
The water is a spray of pinpoints, and the air
is more tender than the frog-skin of air balloons.

[May 1932]

2. 'O, how we love to play the hypocrite'

O, how we love to play the hypocrite,
and how easily we forget,
that in childhood we are nearer death
than in our mature years.

The child who has not slept well
still sucks his indignation from a saucer,
but I have no one to blame,
and wherever I go I'm alone.

The animals moult, the fish play
in the deep swoon of the waters.
O, if only I could be spared from seeing
the painful turns of human passions, human cares.

[May 1932]

3. Lamarck

There was an old man, a clumsy, timid patriarch,
who was as shy as a young boy.
Who was it who fought a duel for nature's honour?
Why, of course, it was fiery Lamarck.

If life is only a correction mark
on a short repossessed day,
then I will be on the last run
on Lamarck's moving ladder.

I'll descend to the worms and the vermin,
scuttling among lizards and snakes,
down the springy gangplank to nature's subdivisions
until I diminish and disappear like Proteus.

I'll become crustaceous,
and cold-blooded,
suckers will grow all over me,
and like a mollusc I will drink the foam of the ocean.

We went past the ranks of insects
with their full wine-glass eyes.
He said: 'Nature is all in chaos,
there's no vision left – you are seeing for the last time.'

He said, 'You've had enough rich harmony,
you loved Mozart in vain.
The spider's deafness is upon us,
the abyss is stronger than our powers.'

Nature has abandoned us,
as though she didn't need us,
and she laid a primeval brain
like a sword into a dark sheath.

She forgot the drawbridge,
it was too late to lower it,
for those who have a green grave,
red breathing, and buoyant laughter.

[7-9 May 1932]

4. 'When Russian gold'

When Russian gold
forced its way into far-off Korea
I ran off into the conservatory
holding an iris to my cheek.

It was the time of erupting laughter,
and swollen thyroid glands,
it was the time of Taras Bulba
and the approaching thunderstorm.

It was the time of decisions and self-will,
and the advance of the Trojan horse.
Over the log-pile was an embassy
of air, sun and fire.

The atmosphere from the bonfires
was thick as sticky crawling caterpillars.
And cheers resounded on the mountain of wood
at the news of Tsushima and of the fortress of St Peter and Paul.

God help us,
we went off, in our high boots,
to the mountain and young prince Chlor,
looking for chloroform.

I've outlived that adolescent,
and my path opens wide before me.
Now I've other dreams and other refuges,
but I'm still a bandit at heart.

[11-13 May 1932]

5. Impressionism

The artist has painted
the deep swoon of lilacs.
He has placed opaque scales on the canvas
which reverberate in steps of colour.

He understood the thick-baked
summeriness of oils,
heated by the lilac brain
to expand into closeness.

And the shadow, ever more lilac,
is it a whistle or a whip, dying like a match.
You'd say, 'the cooks in the kitchen
are preparing plump pigeons.'

You can just barely see a swing
and some veils,
and in the twilight fragmentation
the bumble bees have already settled.

[23 May 1932]

6. 'Remember how the young men'

Remember how the young men
in Verona
raced in the fields
striving to win the green banner.

But the runner in
Dante's book
will run arguments around them
and outrun them all.

[May 1932]

7. Novellino

Remember how Dante's
runners competed in
the spring for the honour
of the green trophy.

In their leather boots
they scattered over hills
and dark velvet meadows
like poppies by the roadside.

Don't mention those garrulous
vagrants, the Florentines to me.
They're a pack of incorrigible liars
and hired murderers.

As the church bells rang
they prayed in a drunken stupor.
They gave hawks as presents
to the Turkish sultan.

But, alas, the candles of the hot-headed
young bloods have burnt out;
those youths, who once swaggered about
in skimpy green undershirts,

who conquered their own guilt
and the plague's affliction
and served many,
different masters.

There's no one left to tell the story
of the women in their long, sinful dresses,
whose days passed like a dream
in ensnaring occupations.

They told fortunes with wax and spun silk
and taught parrots to speak
and let scoundrels into
their bedrooms for pleasure or profit.

[22 May 1932]

8. 'Guess why you've given'

Guess why you've given
Tyutchev a dragonfly,
and a rose to Venevitinov,
but the seal ring is not for anyone.

The soles of Baratynsky's boots
stir up the dust of ages
and he's been granted the seamless
pillowslips of clouds.

Lermontov, soaring free above us,
torments us,
and Fet's fat pencil
is always sick with asthma.

Khomyakov's beard
is preserved by God
to hang on a nail for ever
by the gates of Jerusalem.

[May – July 1932]

9. Batyushkov

Gentle Batyushkov lives with me
like an idler with a magic wand.
He walks down the side streets to Zamostye,
and sniffs a rose and sings of Zafna.

It seems as if we were never apart.
I bowed to him,
and squeezed his cold hand in his bright glove
with feverish envy.

He smiled. I could only thank him,
overcome as I was with embarrassment.
No one has ever had his nuances of tone,
nor his murmuring ebb and flow.

He, in his awkwardness, brought with him
our riches and our torment,
the noise of poetry, the bell of brotherhood,
and tears shed in harmony,

And he, who had mourned Tasso, answered me:
'I'm not yet used to praise,
my language was refreshed by a chance drink
of the wine of lyrics.'

Then raise your eyebrows in surprise
citizen and friend of citizens,
and pour your eternal dreams
like specimens of blood from glass to glass.

[18 June 1932]

10. Poem to Russian Poetry

I

Sit down Derzhavin, make yourself comfortable,
you are a sly fox,
and your yeast has not curdled
the Tartar kumiss.

Pass Yazykov the bottle
and give him a glass.
I love his grin,
the throbbing vein of his intoxication,
and his incandescent poetry.

The thunder lives in its rolling:
why should it concern itself with our troubles?
And the thunder delights in
the taste and colour of muscat
which it swallows with every peal.

Rain drops jump and gallop.
Hailstones race in a herd.
There is a city smell, the smell of a flood,
there is a smell that is neither jasmine,
nor dill, nor oak bark.

II

Moscow and its suburbs
started rustling and quivering
down to its roots,
like the trembling leaves of the fig tree.

The thunder rolls its cart
along the wooden roads,
and the cloudburst paces up and down
with the long lash of streaming rain.

The earth seems
to lean over obsequiously,
as the clouds troop out
in the soft shoes of the executioner.

The rain drops jump and gallop,
hailstones race in a herd.
There is the sweat of slaves, the hoofbeats of horses
and a rumour of trees.

III   *To S.A. Klychkov*

I fell in love with the beautiful
confusing forest, where trumps are clubs;
where there is a red pepper in a maple leaf
and a blue-black hedgehog in the pine needles.

There, pistachio voices
have grown silent on milk,
and when you want to crack them into song
there's no truth on the tongue.

In the forest lives a race of little people,
wearing acorn caps,
and they turn the bloodied white flesh of a squirrel
on the wheel of torture.

In the forest there is a bird's udder, sorrel,
and the peacock blast of pine branches,
confusion and grandeur
and darkness in the nutshell.

The wood-devils with tricorn hats
and long noses poke with their swords.
The executioners read books
by the samovar on coals.

A ripple of mushrooms
in the harness of light rain,
suddenly springs up at the edge of the forest
after having hidden for a time.

On the seventh wave the outcasts
gamble for no profit
The horses snort, the cards are marked –
whose side are you on? The breakdown has happened.

And as the trees rise up,
brother against brother, hurry to understand:
how crude they are,
how very good they are...

[3-7 June 1932]

11.   To the German Language
for B.S. Kuzin

I destroy and contradict myself,
like a moth flying into a lamp's flame at midnight.
I want to go outside our language
because of everything that ties me to it for ever.

Between us there is praise without flattery,
and true friendship without pharisaism.
Let us study seriousness and honour
in the West in a foreign family.

Poetry, storms are useful to you!
I remember Kleist, the German officer.
Roses twined round the hilt of his sword,
and Ceres was always on his lips.

Long before Goethe had been heard of,
the Frankfurt elders yawned,
hymns were composed, and the horses pranced
like letters dancing on the page.

Friends, in what Valhalla
did we crack nuts together?
What freedom did we have,
and what landmarks have you put up for me?

Straight from the novelty
of the first pages of an almanac,
we vanished into the grave as into a wine cellar
for a glass of Moselle.

A foreign language will be my sanctuary;
as long before I dared to be born,
I was a letter, I was a line in a vineyard,
I was a book you dreamed.

When I slept without form or logic,
I was awoken by friendship as if by a gunshot.
God of the Nightingale, give me Pylades' fate,
or tear out my tongue – I don't need it.

God of the Nightingale, they still recruit me
for new plagues, for Seven Year massacres.
The sound has narrowed, the words hiss and mutiny,
but you are alive, and with you I'm at peace.

[8-12 August 1932]

12. 'Old Crimea'

It's a cold spring. The Crimea is starving and fearful
and as guilty as it was with Vrangel and the White Guard.
The patched rags are in tatters, the sheepdogs are in the yard,
and the smoke is biting and pungent as ever.

The views are hazy, it is as beautiful as ever.
The trees are in bud, swelling slightly,
and are the real outsiders, and the almond,
blossoming with yesterday's foolishness, arouses pity.

Nature can't recognise her own face:
the refugees from the Kuban and the Ukraine are nightmare shadows.
The hungry villagers in their felt slippers
guard the storehouse gates, never touching the locks.

[May 1933]

13. Ariosto

Ariosto, the most pleasant, intelligent man in the whole of Italy
has gone a little hoarse.
He loves to name all the fish,
and pepper the seas with the most wicked absurdity.

Like a musician with ten cymbals
he leads the complex plot about knightly scandals
hither and thither, forever breaking
the music of narration.

He uses the language of the cicadas which is a fascinating mixture
of Pushkinian sadness and Mediterranean arrogance.
He is an incorrigible liar, playing tricks on Orlando,
and shudders and changes completely.

He says to the sea: 'Roar without thought!'
And to the maiden on the rock: 'Lie down without a covering...'
Tell us some more, we have too little of you,
while we have blood in our veins, and roaring in our ears...

Ferrara, you're a harsh town of lizards; there is no soul in you.
If only you would produce such men more often.
While we have blood in our veins
hurry and tell the story once more from the beginning.

It's cold in Europe and dark in Italy.
Power is as disgusting as the hands of a barber.
He plays the great man with increasing skill and cunning,
smiling from the open window,

at the lamb on the mountain, the monk on a donkey,
at the duke's soldiers, slightly simple-minded
with wine, and plague, and garlic,
and at the child dozing under a net of blue flies.

And I love his furious leisure,
his bitter-sweet stream of consciousness.
I'm afraid to pry out of the double-hinged shell
the pearl made of beautiful twin layers of sound.

Dear Ariosto, perhaps this age will pass –
and we'll blend your Mediterranean and our Black Sea
together into one brotherly blue expanse.
We've been there too, and we have drunk mead.

[4-6 May 1933]

14. 'It's cold in Europe, and dark in Italy'

It's cold in Europe, and dark in Italy.
Power is as disgusting as the hands of a barber.
If only a wide window onto the Adriatic
could be quickly thrown open.

A bee buzzes over a musk rose,
a muscular grasshopper is in the southern wasteland,
the shoes of the winged horse are heavy,
and the sands of the hour-glass are golden.

He uses the language of the cicadas which is a fascinating mixture
of Pushkinian sadness and Mediterranean arrogance.
He lies bravely, like ivy
clinging everywhere, playing tricks on Orlando.

The sands of the hour glass are golden,
there is a muscular grasshopper in the sourthern wasteland,
and the broad-shouldered liar flies straight to the moon.

Dear Ariosto, embassy fox,
flowering fern, tall ship, agave,
you listened to the voices of the yellow birds on the moon,
and were a wise counsellor to the fish at court.

Ferrara, you are a rough city of lizards which has no soul.
The witches and judges of rough Ferrara
gave birth to such sons and kept them shackled.
The red-headed sun rose over the wild land.

We're amazed by the butcher's stall,
the child dozing under a net of blue flies,
the lamb on the mountain, the monk on the donkey,
by the duke's soldiers, slightly simple-minded
with wine, plague, and garlic,
and amazed by loss, fresh as the dawn.

[4-6 May 1933 / July 1935]

15. 'Don't tempt yourself with foreign languages'

Don't tempt yourself with foreign languages – try to forget them:
after all you won't be able to bite through glass with your teeth.

O, how tormenting is the flight of a strange bird's scream,
you pay a harsh penalty for illicit pleasures.

At the final parting a foreign name will not save
the dying body and the thinking, eternal mouth.

What if Ariosto and Tasso, who enchant us, who enchant us,
are monsters with blue brains and scaly, wet eyes.

In punishment for your arrogance, you incorrigible lover of sounds,
you'll receive the sponge soaked in vinegar for your treacherous lips.

16. 'The friend of Ariosto'

The friend of Ariosto, friend of Petrarch, Tasso's friend –
used the bitter-sweet stream of consciousness.
I'm afraid to pry out of the double-hinged shell
the pearl made of beautiful twin layers of sound.

17. 'The flat is quiet as paper'

The flat is quiet as paper,
empty, without any ornaments.
One can hear the moisture bubbling
in the radiators.

Everything is in order.
The phone sits still like a frozen frog.
Our possessions, who have seen it all,
want to be on the move again.

And the cursed walls are thin,
and there's nowhere left to run,
and I'm forced to entertain someone,
like a fool playing a comb.

More brazen than a Komsomol cell
more brazen than a student song,
I teach bird calls
to the executioners perched on the school bench.

I read rationed books,
and catch fragments of demagogue speeches,
and sing a menacing lullaby
to the child of the *kulak*.

Some realist writer,
comber of the collective farm's flax,
someone with blood in his ink
deserves such a hell.

After the purges are boiled away,
some honest traitor
is left like salt around the edges,
a good family man who will take a swipe at a moth like me.

How much torture and anger
is hidden in each veiled hint,
as though Nekrasov's hammer
were smashing in nails in my walls.

Come on now, it's time for you to put your head on the block,
you're seventy years old,
you slovenly old man,
it's time for you to put your boots on.

It's not the ancient spring of Hippocrene,
which will burst through the cardboard walls,
but the gush of age-old terror
which will flood this evil Moscow home.

[Furmanov backstreet, Moscow, November 1933]

18. 'Our sacred youth'

Our sacred youth
have good songs in their blood;
songs like lullabies
battle cries against feudal landlords.

But I watch over myself
and sing something like this:
rock a bye despots of collective farms
and lullaby the *kulak*'s child.

[November 1933]

19. 'The Tartars, Uzbeks and Nentsians'

The Tartars, Uzbeks and Nentsians,
all the Ukrainian people,
even the Volga Germans,
are waiting for their interpreters.

And perhaps at this very moment,
some Japanese is translating
me into Turkish,
and has penetrated deep into my soul.

[November 1933]

20. 'We are alive but no longer feel'

We are alive but no longer feel the land under our feet,
you can't hear what we say from ten steps away,

but when anyone half-starts a conversation
they mention the mountain man of the Kremlin.

His thick fingers are like worms,
his words ring as heavy weights.

His cockroach moustache laughs,
and the tops of his tall boots shine.

He is surrounded by his scrawny necked henchmen,
and plays with the services of non-entities.

Someone whistles, someone miaows and another whimpers,
he alone points at us and thunders.

He forges order after order like horseshoes,
hurling them at the groin, the forehead, the brow, the eye.

The broad-breasted boss from the Caucasus
savours each execution like an exquisite sweet.

[November 1933]

21. Octets

I

I love how the cloth appears,
when after two or three or
maybe even four gasps of air
an expansive sigh comes,

and space, drawing green forms
with the sweeping arcs of racing sailing boats
plays, half-asleep,
like a child that never knew the cradle.

II

I love how the cloth appears,
when after two or three or
maybe even four gasps of air
an expansive sigh comes,
I feel so good, so concentrated,
as the moment approaches
and suddenly, out of my mumblings
sounds fill out and stretch.

III

When you've destroyed all the rough drafts,
and you hold a sentence in your mind
steadfastly, without tedious references,
integral in inner darkness,
when that sentence stands up on its own,
opening its eyes, that were squinting in concentration,
then its relationship to the paper
is the same as that of the dome to the empty skies.

IV

O butterfly, O Moslem woman,
in your gaping shroud,
living and dying
so grandly.
You bite, and with your long antennae
you thrust your head into the burnous.
O shroud, unfurled like a flag.
Fold your wings. I'm afraid.

V

Schubert on the water and Mozart in the birds' chatter,
Goethe whistling on a twisting path,
and Hamlet, who paced his thoughts in fear,
all took the pulse of the crowd and trusted in it.

Perhaps the whisper was born before the lips,
the leaves circled and fell before the forest,
and those to whom we dedicate our experience
had acquired their qualities before the experience.

VI

Tell me, surveyor of the desert,
geometer of the Arabian sands,
is the unbridled freedom of lines
more powerful than the blowing wind?
'The tremble of his Jewish worries
doesn't concern me.
He creates experience from his babbling
and drinks babbling from experience.'

VII

The serrated leaves on the maple branch
bathe in the round corners of the sky,
and one could cover the walls with paintings
made of the colour flecks of butterflies.
There are mosques that are alive,
and I have just now realised:
perhaps we are the Cathedral of Haghia Sophia
with an infinite multitude of eyes.

VIII

The tiny attribute of sixth sense,
the eye in the crown of the lizard,
the monasteries of snails and shells,
the flickering little conversation of antennae:
the unobtainable is so close!
You cannot decipher or observe it,
as if a note had been pressed in your hand
that you must answer at once.

IX

Beyond the fossilised lessons of nature
the hard blue eye penetrates its law.
The rock plays the holy fool as the ore tears itself
from within the earth's crust, like a groan from the chest,
and the insentient foetus stretches
like a road, which bends into the shape of a horn,
trying to grasp the abundance of inner space
and the pledge of the petal and the dome.

X

We drink the delusion of causality,
from the fluted champagne glasses of the plague.
We hook onto magnitudes
small as an easy death.
The child keeps its silence
in face of the jumbled pile of pick-up-sticks.
The big universe sleeps in the cradle
rocked by the small eternity.

XI

I go out from space
into the overgrown garden of multitudes,
and pluck false constancy
and self-consciousness of causality.
In solitude,
I read your texts, infinity:
a wild leafless book of healing,
a book of problems with huge roots.

[May 1932 – July 1935]

22. 'The forest birds could tell of this'

'Valle che de' lamenti miei se' piena...'

The forest birds could tell of this,
the stream, swollen from salty tears,
the sensitive beasts and dumb fish
squeezed between two green banks.

The valley, full of promises and burning whispers,
the meandering curves of well-trodden paths,
the rock masses fossilised by the power of love,
and the cracks in the earth on the difficult slopes.

The firmest and most unshakable places are quaking,
and I am shaken. As though mourning is embedded
in the very granite in the nest of former happinesses.

Here I search for the traces of beauty and honour,
which have disappeared, like a hawk after it's torn its prey,
and left its body to lie in the earth's bed.

23. 'An orphaned nightingale sings'

'Quel rosignuol che si soave piagne...'

An orphaned nightingale sings
of its close family in the blue night,
and he melts the silence of the countryside
over the hills and valleys.

All night long he tickles me,
and alone for evermore accompanies me.
He traps me and snares me and compels me
to remember the death sweat of the goddess.

O, the iris of terror! The earth took
the ether of eyes that had looked into the depths of the atmosphere
into the blind cradle of dust and ashes.

The spinner's wish was fulfilled,
and I repeat as I cry: all the world's beauty
is less eternal than the flicker of an eyelash.

[December 1933 – January 1934]

24.   'My days have raced past'

'I di miel più legier che nessun cervo...'

My days have raced past like the sloping
run of deer. The time of happiness was briefer
than the flicker of an eyelash. Out of one final effort
I squeezed only a handful of the ashes of delight.

The heart sleeps in the crypt of the modest night,
at the mercy of grandiose delusions,
and presses into the boneless earth.
It seeks familiar focusses, and sweet intertwinings.

But what scarcely existed in her,
now having escaped upwards into the hearth of the azure sky,
can capture and wound as before.

And as I frown in consternation, I guess at
how beautiful she is, at what crowd she is with,
and at the storm of light folds swirling there.

25. 'When the earth sleeps'

'Or che 'l ciel e la terra e 'l vento face...'

When the earth sleeps, and the heat dies down,
and the swan's peace glides into the soul of beasts,
night circles with burning yarn,
and zephyrs sway the powerful waves:

I feel, burn, strain and cry: but she does not hear,
she's the same in her irrepressible closeness,
all night through I watch her,
and she breathes in her distant happiness as before.

The water speaks of a contradiction, though the spring is the same –
both hard and sweet:
is my darling two-faced in the same way?

A thousand times a day,
I amaze myself by dying in reality,
and rising again in the same extraordinary way.

26. 'As water flows'

As water flows from
one high mountain crevice, a contradiction to the taste,
both hard and sweet, two-faced,

so, to die in reality,
a thousand times a day, I shall be deprived
of the common freedom of breathing, and knowing there is a purpose.

27. 'You had blue eyes and a feverish brow'

You had blue eyes and a feverish brow.
The invigorating malice of the world attracted you.

And since you were endowed with magical powers
they decided never to judge or curse you.

They crowned you, but it was with the cap of the holy fool,
turquoise teacher, torturer, tyrant, jester.

You herded your words like a gaggle of ducks into Moscow,
a snowstorm, dense, impenetrable and luminous.

You are a collector of space, a fledgling graduate,
author, young goldfinch, student, little student, jester's bell…

skater and first son of an age that hurled you out by the scruff
of the neck onto the frosty dust of word spinning.

One often writes 'Execution', and means, 'Song':
perhaps simplicity is a sickness which can be wounded to death.

Honesty is not a toy gun pointed only at children,
it's not the paper that saves people, but the news.

As dragonflies, not touching the water, settle on reeds,
so the fat pencils swarmed round the dead man

Holding their sketch pads they drew for generations to come,
apologising to every line.

An icy bond is forming between you and this country,
so lie there and grow young, stretching into eternity,

and let the young generations of the future never ask:
'How do you feel there, you orphan, in your clean void?'

[10-11 January 1934]

81

28. 'A few random phrases keep haunting me'

A few random phrases keep haunting me.
All day I repeat: 'the richness of my sadness.'
Oh God, the dragonflies of death are black, and their eyes
are so blue, and the blue sky so absolutely black.

Where is the first-born's birthright, where is the joyful tradition?
Or the tiny hawk that floats in the depths of the eye?
Where is civility or the bitterness of deception?
Where is the clear figure? Or straight talk

complex as a skater's honest zigzags?
The skates flame blue:
do the blades whirl in the pull of dusty ice
clinking glasses with the hard, blue river?

The engraver's solution made from three different salts,
the voices of the wise German philosophers,
and the brilliant arguments of Russia's heirs,
made half a century into half an hour for him.

Suddenly the music staged an ambush,
no longer flying from the violin bows like birds of prey,
not for listening, nor for pleasure,
but flowing for the muscles and pounding temples.

It flows for the tender death mask, just removed,
for the plaster fingers which hold no pen,
for the swollen lips, and for the tight embrace
of coarse-grained peace and goodness.

*　　*　　*

The fur of overcoats breathed. Shoulder pressed against shoulder.
Rude health boiled over – blood and sweat.
You sleep, enveloped in a dream in which you sought
to move forward half a step.

An engraver was in the crowd
offering to transfer onto pure copper
what the draftsman could only begin
as a charcoal sketch on paper.

I may hang on my own eyelashes,
ripening and swelling, acting out
all the parts in the play until I run.
The plot's the only thing we know today.

[January 1934]

29. 'When fate suddenly confronts'

When fate suddenly confronts
the timid, hastening soul,
it runs down the twisted path;
but death's road is not easy to follow.

It seems that he was shy of dying
with the appealing modesty of a novice,
or the first sound to echo round a brilliant gathering,
which flows into the linear forest of violin bows.

And so, the sound of the bow flows, on and back lazily,
measuring itself by the length of flax, by the length of filaments,
resinous, hardly believing that it flows
from nothing, from a thread, from darkness.

It flows for the tender death mask, just removed,
for the plaster fingers which hold no pen,
for the swollen lips, and for the tight embrace
of coarse-grained peace and goodness.

[January 1934]

30. 'Who died?'

Where was he brought from? Who? Who was it who died?
Where will they bury him? I'm not quite sure.
They say that some Gogol's died,
well not exactly Gogol, just some writer...a little Gogol duck.

The same bright, amusing man
who cultivated absurdity,
was absent-minded, couldn't grasp some things,
organised bedlam and hurled snowballs.

He's as silent as an oyster now. You cannot
get closer to him than a couple of yards – his guard of honour won't
        let you.
Something's being covered up for some reason.
.   .   .   .   .   . he just got confused and fell asleep.

[10 January 1934]

31. 'He conducted the Caucasus mountains'

He conducted the Caucasus mountains.
Waving his arms he went up the paths of the dense Alps,
and looking round, on the deserted shores
he walked, sensing the conversation of the huge crowd.

He brought across – as only a powerful man could have –
a crowd of minds, events and impressions.
Rachel looked for revelations in the mirror,
and Leah wove her wreath and sang.

[January 1934]

32. 'The Caucasus mountains'

The Caucasus mountains and the crowd of the tender Alps
that blocked the way, shouted to him,
His visionary footsteps mounted
the steep choruses of mountains of sound.

He brought across – as only a powerful man could have,
the burgeoning of European thought,
Rachel looked for revelations in the mirror,
and Leah wove her wreath and sang.

33. 'A bearded engraver'

A bearded engraver was already standing in the crowd, lost in thought.
A friend of copper and pine plates which are flooded
by three kinds of oxide until they gleam
and the surface of truth shines through the wax.

It was like hanging by my own eyelashes:
the air was crowded with winged angels from the paintings
of those masters, who put vision into faces
and order of the liturgy into crowds.

34. 'For Maria Petrovykh'

The expert mistress of guilty glances
who has such slender shoulders.
subdues the male's dangerous obstinacy,
and drowns his words.

The fish are fluttering their fins as they swim,
puffing out their gills. Take them,
mouthing their soundless 'O's,
feed them the half-bread of flesh.

We're not goldfish.
Ours is the fellowship of sisters,
the warm body's frail ribs,
and the vain sparkle of moist eyes.

The sweep of your eyebrows describes a dangerous path.
Am I really in love as a Turkish soldier
would be, with the vulnerable, red crescent
of your small capricious lips?

Don't be angry with me, dear Turkish woman,
I'll sew myself up in a sack with you,
swallowing your dark words,
drinking the crooked water for you.

You, Maria, are the help of those who are perishing.
One must anticipate death, and fall asleep.
I'm standing at your harsh threshold,
Go away. Please go now. Please stay.

[February 1934]

Notes

1. *The Noise of Time*, translated by Clarence Brown (Quartet Encounter, new edition, 1985). Clarence Brown has also written a biography and commentary on the earlier poems, *Mandelstam* (Cambridge University Press, 1973).

2. Nadezhda Mandelstam: *Hope Against Hope*, p.232. Nadezhda Mandelstam's *Hope Against Hope* and *Hope Abandoned*, both translated by Max Hayward, were first published by Atheneum Publishers (USA) and by Harvill Press, and then in paperback by Penguin Books, and are now published by Collins Harvill. Osip Mandelstam's *Critical Prose and Letters*, edited by Jane Gary Harris, which includes the *Journey to Armenia*, was published by Ardis in 1979 and then by Collins Harvill in Britain in 1991.

ESSAY BY VICTOR KRIVULIN

'a jump and I am back in my mind': a quotation from 'Stanzas', written in Voronezh, after he had recovered from a suicide attempt in psychiatric hospital in Cherdyn, after a sleepless train journey with Nadezhda into exile from Moscow, where he had been held and interrogated in the Lubyanka. See Nadezhda Mandelstam's *Hope Against Hope* (Penguin/Collins Harvill editions, pp.68-89).

FIRST MOSCOW NOTEBOOK

1. This poem that broke the five year silence was written in September-October 1930, in Tiflis, Georgia, at the end of the Mandelstams' eight-month trip to Armenia, to his wife Nadezhda Yakovlevna, round about the time of her Name Day on 30 September. The nut pie is her "birthday" cake.

The Armenian Group: 2-8.

2. II. Mandelstam wrote in *Journey to Armenia*: 'The teeth of vision crumble and break up when you encounter Armenian churches for the first time' (*Critical Prose*, p.372).

II. l.5. 'pedlars'': *moskatelny* in the Russian, has a colourfulness in it, whether of paints or the colours of the Armenian terrain.

'sardars': Persian and Turkish rulers. In *Journey to Armenia*, Mandelstam says about a Persian pencil case: 'I wanted to smell its venerable musty panels which had served Sardar justice and the invoking of instantaneous sentences to put men's eyes out' (*Critical Prose*, p.356).

'young tombs': the Armenian massacres were only ten or fifteen years before the Mandelstams' visit to Armenia. See note to 'The Horse-cart Driver' (I. 28).

IV. On his death bed Pushkin asked for frozen grapes.

V. Rose oil was so valuable it was almost a currency.

VIII. Lake Sevan is a lake high in the mountains of Armenia that the Mandelstams visited. Echmiadzin has an ancient Armenian-Gregorian monastery near Erevan.

Ararat: from *Journey to Armenia*: 'I have cultivated a sixth sense in myself, an "Ararat" sense; I can feel the mountain's gravitational pull' (*Critical Prose*, p.372).

IX. Khardzhiev mentions that Mandelstam has in mind the Yezidic Kurds with their mixture of Christianity, Islam, and the ancient Iranian belief in the equal power of good and evil.

3. (Last stanza) from *Journey to Armenia*: 'Stupid vanity and sense of false pride held me back from berry-picking as a child, nor did I ever stoop to pick mushrooms. I preferred the Gothic pine cone and hypocritical acorns' (*Critical Prose*, p.355).

5. An earlier draft, quoted by I. Semenko, is helpful in establishing the meaning of 'mustard': 'But the lifeless plaster of the lands/ is a grey-green mustard poultice.'

'face like a gun': the Russian word is *tufyak*, traditionally translated as 'mattress', indicating flabbiness; however in Turkish and Farsi *tufek* or *tufang* are a gun.

8. 'RAPP reports': The powerful Russian Association of Proletarian Writers, disbanded in 1932.

The Leningrad Poems: 9-12.

9. 'dear guests': the NKVD (forerunners of the KGB).

12. Mandelstam concealed this poem from Nadezhda.

13. 'silvery mouse': A reference to Pushkin's poem 'Lines Written in a Sleepless Night': 'the mouselike scurrying of life'.

14. The epigraph *'Ma voix aigre et fausse'* comes from the Verlaine poem 'Sérènade' from his 1866 book *Poèmes Saturniens*: '(my mistress, hear) my bitter, false voice'. It is likely that Mandelstam's 'Angel Mary' refers both to Nadezhda Mandelstam and to Mary,

the singer in Pushkin's *Feast in the Time of the Plague*. 'sherry brandy' Mandelstam made up to mean 'nonsense'.

15. 'The Wolf': The Yenisey river in Siberia was also used, almost symbolically, by Anna Akhmatova in her *Requiem*. Despite Siberia's historical and contemporary associations with concentration camps it appeared to Mandelstam almost as a welcome refuge.

Fragments from 'The Wolf Cycle'

1

The newspaper spits up something that is not tobacco blood,
the girl taps but not with her knuckles –
the hot, disfigured, human mouth
is indignant and says 'no'...

2

...The monkish workers walked ahead
like mischievous children.
The blue polar foxes and the palaces and prisons,
only one powerful person sings...

3

The ink of the mud of Moscow turned to gold,
and a lorry grunted by the gates,
and the dense crowd, writing themselves into history
surged down the streets to the palaces and prisons.

[Reminscences of 1917]

4

But when I hear that voice, I shall go for an axe
and finish his story myself.

5

Be quiet! Never say anything to anyone –
time is singing there in the fire...

6

Be quiet! I no longer believe in anything:
I am a pedestrian just like you,
but your threatening, disfigured mouth
returns me to my shame.

7

Take me off into the night, where the Yenisey flows
and the tears on the eyelashes are ice,
My blood is not the blood of a wolf
and in me the man will not die.

8

Take me off into the night, where the Yenisey flows,
take away my pride and my work –
my blood is not the blood of a wolf
and others will come after me.

16. Nadezhda Mandelstam asserts this poem is in reaction to Pasternak's poem of 1931 (*Pasternak Collected Works* [in Russian] vol 1, (Michigan, 1961), p.341), and especially the lines: 'Rhyme is not an echo of a line/ but a ticket to hang one's coat in the cloakroom,/ a voucher for a place by the columns...'

17. The musician used to practise nextdoor to Mandelstam's brother's Moscow flat where the Mandelstams were staying temporarily.

18. Mandelstam was particularly fond of prison songs.

20. There was a rumour that Stalin had six toes (or fingers), but the main impulse of the poem is its almost folkloric horror. A rough draft fragment from the 'Wolf Cycle' links this poem with 'The Wolf':

Take me off into the night, where the Yenisey flows,
to the six-toed untruth in the hut,
because my blood is not the blood of a wolf,
after all I too will have to lie in a pine coffin.

21. 'Asters': this is often translated as 'epaulettes'.

22. The poem deals partly with an unsuccessful concert by the pianist Heinrich Neuhaus.
Sweet potato, literally a sweet *'poire de terre'* or as Mandelstam commented impatiently 'just a frozen potato'.

23. In the last line Mandelstam is referring, as in II. 14. to Peter the Great.

24. 'Canzone': This poem is discussed in detail in 'The Power of Vision', in *Hope Abandoned* (Ch.35.x). The crimson embrace refers to the suffusion of red in Rembrandt's picture *Prodigal Son* in the Hermitage in Leningrad.

27. Included in these fragments were the lines 'and women's fingers smell of kerosene/ and blood spurts from kitchen sinks'.

28. The Russian word spelt in the text *araba* means 'of an Arab', but it is also a widespread Turkish/Azerbaijani word for 'horse cart'. In 1920 the Armenian population of Shusha in Nagorno Karabakh were massacred.

29. Last stanza: although there is a pencil note on the 'Vatican Codex' manuscript that this stanza should go here, and it is included in the body of the poems of the Merani Edition, Nadezhda Mandelstam goes on record in the Voronezh University Edition as saying: 'The Tartar backs are glistening': He [Mandelstam] rejected without any hesitation because of the last line. 'It's something completely different,' he said. To put it another way, the lads by the river for a first, touching moment appeared to him to be the basis of life, but he knew perfectly well that they were as slenderly connected to what was going on as himself.

30. In the most recent Soviet editions this stanza is included second from the end of the poem:

I love the squeaking tram trips
and the Astrakhan caviar of asphalt,
covered with straw matting,
reminiscent of the baskets of Asti Spumante
and the ostrich feathers of scaffolding
at the Lenin building sites.

SECOND MOSCOW NOTEBOOK

3. 'Lamarck': the French naturalist Jean Baptiste Lamarck. From Around the Naturalists in *Journey to Armenia*: 'Lamarck fought sword in hand for the honour of living nature...In Lamarck's reversed, descending movement down the ladder of living creatures, there is a greatness worthy of Dante. The lower forms of organic existence are the hell of humanity' (*Critical Prose*, p.366).
Grigory Freidin, in his book on Mandelstam, *A Coat of Many Colours* (Berkeley, 1988), advances the original and extraordinary idea that the 'moving ladder/staircase' is, subliminally perhaps, the escalator of the Moscow Underground that was being built at the time.

4. This poem is an integration of Mandelstam's boyhood years. It is remarkable for its concentration on heroic ventures or disasters, and its Eastern settings: Korea, Tsushima, Khlor, Troy, brought in via schoolbook writers Gogol (Taras Bulba), Homer and Derzhavin (Khlor). Tsushima was where the Russian fleet was defeated in the Russo-Japanese War in 1905. Derzhavin's Prince Khlor, in the poems 'Felitsa' and 'To Prince Khlor', is sent off by the Kirghiz Khan who has abducted him to find a rose without thorns. The first version of the opening line of the last stanza originally read: 'I have outlived the sicknesses of growing up'.

5. 'Impressionism': Jennifer Baines (p.58) mentions three paintings (all in Moscow art galleries which Mandelstam loved to visit – see 'The French' in his *Journey to Armenia*) that Mandelstam may have had in mind: Monet's *Lilas au soleil*, and Pissarro's *Boulevard Montmartre* and *Place du Théâtre Français, Printemps*.

6-7. Mandelstam in a theme of (his own) rejuvenation and craftiness is referring to the master, Brunetto Latini – Dante, end of *Inferno* canto XV.

8. The only mention of a dragonfly in the 19th century poet Tyutchev is the verse:

> In the stifling silent air,
> like the forewarning of a storm
> the rose's fragrance is hotter,
> the dragonfly's voice rings louder.

Alexander Pushkin (probable owner of the seal ring/talisman) was sacred to Mandelstam, a constant, but often unmentioned, presence and influence.

9. Zamostye is a town in Eastern Poland. Zafna: from Batyushkov's poem 'The Spring'. Batyushkov (1787-1855) became permanently insane in 1821. Torquato Tasso (1544-1595): Italian poet, to whom Batyushkov dedicated a poem.

10. Mandelstam was at this time much more involved with 19th and late 18th century Russian poetry (and his Italians) than with contemporary poetry. Despite his poverty in Moscow, he was able to collect many first editions of these poets, some of whom are mentioned in this poem and II.8. 'You know, if ever there was a golden age, it was the nineteenth century, only we didn't know.' Mandelstam to Nadezhda at the beginning of the thirties (*Hope Against Hope*, p.253).

11. Mandelstam met the biologist B.S. Kuzin, to whom this poem is dedicated, in Armenia. Kuzin loved German poetry, but argued with Mandelstam about this poem. Mandelstam was more drawn to conversations with scientists than with other poets at this time. In a letter (quoted by Khardzhiev) with the MS of *Journey to Armenia* Mandelstam wrote this accolade to Kuzin: 'My new prose is suffused with his personality, as is all this recent period of my work. I am indebted to him, and him alone for bringing into literature the period of the "mature Mandelstam".'

Christian Kleist (German officer in the original), Romantic poet, served in the Prussian army, died in the Seven Year War battle with the Russians at Kunserdorf. Pylades, Orestes' brother, is symbolic of friendship.

12. Old Crimea: variant 'the bullet-riddled views are still good'. The people, especially the refugees from the Kuban and the Ukraine, in Old Crimea after collectivisation and the failure of the First Five Year Plan were starved and in desperate straits. There, however, Mandelstam met Andrey Bely again, and wrote *Conversation about Dante*, and immersed himself in the Italian poets.

13. Ariosto (1474-1533), poet and author of *Orlando Furioso*, son of a judge, also carried out diplomatic missions for Ferrara.

14. This metaphor of throwing open a window has a parallel in Pushkin's 'Bronze Horseman', where Peter the Great (who is probably also the 'barber') declares his desire, that Petersburg be a window onto the West.

Mandelstam has described the agave in *Journey to Armenia* 'in the park the flowering agave [giant cactus] plants, like candles weighing six poods, shot up a couple of inches every day'.

'kept them shackled': Tasso was locked up in a mental hospital for seven years as a result of a court intrigue.

The last line 'We've been there too, and we have drunk mead', a quotation from Pushkin's *Ruslan and Ludmilla*, is perhaps like Alexander Pope's drinking 'deep of the Pierian (Delphic) spring.'

15. Mandelstam's cautionary (and guilty) poem to himself (and translators) on the foreign languages he loved.

17. Mandelstam's response to Pasternak's comment 'Now you've got a flat you can write poetry.'

Nekrasov: the socialistic poet of the 19th century.

Hippocrene: the classical spring created by Pegasus's hoof. Klyuev had written a dangerous poem 'the Revilers of Art', that both Akhmatova and Mandelstam knew: 'The wolf's jaws, the rack, the mines/ none of these could invent more treacherous tortures/ for the Russian Pegasus in the stone quarry.'

18. According to Nadezhda Mandelstam, Mandelstam kept mixing up *Bay* (feudal landlord – again a Turkish word) and *Pay* (boy). The *kulaks* were successfully collectivised, sent to labour camps or exterminated. The fact that *bay* (pronounced *bye*) is an integral part of a lullaby in Russian and English does not make it any easier for the translator.

20. 'Epigram to Stalin': Mandelstam read this poem to a number of people (not all together). One of them informed on him and it

reached the Kremlin with this couplet: 'You can only hear the mountain man of the Kremlin,/ the mass-murderer and peasant-slayer' from an earlier version. The epigram was his passport to exile – and death.

21. Octets. These poems, possibly part of a long work-to-be, on the subjects of composition, architecture, cognition, geology, evolution, and eternity stand out from the book for their taut structure. The 'fluted' glasses are, in the Russian, as sharp as needles, and again Mandelstam is harking back to Pushkin's *The Feast in the Time of the Plague*.

22-26. *The Petrarch Group*:
Mandelstam's versions of the Petrarchan Sonnets are Mandelstam poems in their own right, and we rightly place them in the *Moscow Notebooks*. They are from *Canzoniere*, CCCI: 22, CLXIV: 24; from *In Vita di Madonna Laura*; *La Morte di Madonna Laura*, CCCXI: 23 and CCCXIX: 25. 'In his versions of Petrarch's work Mandelstam strengthened the emotional force and removed a great deal of the "dolce" element' (Baines, p.100). There is a myth of Mandelstam reading Petrarch aloud round a campfire on his way to the Gulag.

27-33 *Requiem to Bely*:
Mandelstam also envisaged this group of poems as his own Requiem. 'Bely's death made him visualise the possibility that he would be thrown unceremoniously into a hole in the ground, with none of the last respects or funeral rites then being accorded to Bely.' (Baines, p.103). He had become friendly with Bely, the brilliant poet and prose writer, in 1933, when he was writing his *Talking About Dante*. Earlier he had criticised his Symbolist poetry. Much play is made in these Mandelstam poems on the word *gogol*, 'a black and white diving duck of the northern regions', leading into Gogol, and Vyacheslav Ivanov's nickname for Bely, 'Gogolyok', a little duck, or a little Gogol.

27. 'cap of the holy fool': a reference, according to Khardzhiev, to Bely's 1903 poem 'Eternal Call': 'The fool falls silent,/ full of joyous torments./ The madman's cap/ falls quietly to the floor.'

31. Victor Krivulin, in an epigraph he wrote to his poem 'Rapprochement', elucidates the first line of this poem to Bely: 'Witnesses of Andrei Bely's death told that in his last minutes of life, the poet clearly felt that he only had to stretch his hands out to touch the Caucasus mountains with his fingers.'

33. The engraver at the funeral was Favorsky, who illustrated the *Lay of Igor the Great* the early Russian epic, which was a favourite of Mandelstam's.

34. Anna Akhmatova gave the nickname 'The Turkish Woman' to this poem to Maria Petrovykh, a poet and translator she rated highly.

I am grateful for help with these notes to the Nadezhda Mandelstam books, to Jennifer Baines (for her book and conversations about Mandelstam at Oxford in the 60s), to I. Semenko's *The Poetics of Late Mandelstam* (Rome, 1986), especially for her discussion of variants, to the Struve Filipoff American Mandelstam Notes, to the notes of Khardzhiev in the very incomplete 1973 Biblioteka Edition of Osip Mandelstam, and to the Tallinn edition of Mandelstam 1989, edited by Pavel Nerler, which, although it has very few notes, includes all the later poems, and some variants; and for discussions with Peter Norman, Sir Dimitri Obolensky and with Russian friends, especially the poets Victor Krivulin, Dimitri Vedenyapin and Alla Gelich. The quotations from *Journey to Armenia* are from *Osip Mandelstam: Critical Prose and Letters*, edited by Jane Gary Harris (Collins Harvill, 1991).

When this book was already in proof, I managed to obtain copies of *Osip Mandelstam: Poems, Translations, Essays and Articles*, edited by G.G. Margelashvili and P.M. Nerler (Merani, Tiflis, 1990), and the more scholarly *Life and Art of Osip Mandelstam*, edited by S.S. Averintsev and P.M. Nerler and others (Voronezh University, 1990), which concentrates on *The Moscow Notebooks* and *The Voronezh Notebooks*, with commentary by Nadezhda Mandelstam and I. Semenko, and articles by various hands. It is a credit to Western scholars, and to the accuracy of the texts brought out of the Soviet Union, that there are no more than two dozen or so textual changes from the American Struve and Filipoff 1967 edition. These we were able to incorporate into our translation, and are happy that the publication of our edition of *The Moscow Notebooks* coincides so appositely with the large-scale publication of Osip Mandelstam's later poetry in his own country, and in his centenary year.   RMcK.

ERRATA

INTRODUCTIONS

page 11, *l.* 13: *for:* Vaselovo; *read:* Savelovo.

page 13, *l.* 26: *for:* a matter; *read:* the matter.

page 17, *l.* 11: *for:* persuading himself ordering himself; *read:* persuading himself, ordering himself.

POEMS

page 27, 2. 'Armenia', IV, *l.* 8: *for:* they take; *read:* and they take.

page 38, 15. 'The Wolf', *l.* 1: *for:* I have forsaken my place at the feast of my fathers; *read:* I have been deprived of the chalice at the feast of the fathers.

page 38, 15. 'The Wolf', *l.* 9: *for:* débris; *read:* quaking.

page 43, 22. The Grand Piano, *l.* 2: *insert comma after:* discord.

page 59, 4. 'When Russian gold', *ll.* 6-7: *for:* It was the time of erupting laughter,/ and swollen thyroid glands; *read:* It was the time of funny Adam's apples,/ and bulbous thyroid glands.

page 59, 4. 'When Russian gold', *l.* 16: *for:* at the news of Tsushima and of the fortress of St Peter and Paul; *read:* at the flagship going to Tsushima.

page 71, 15. 'Don't tempt yourself with foreign languages', *l.* 7: *for:* who enchant us, who enchant us; *read:* who enchant us.

page 81, 27. 'You had blue eyes and a feverish brow', *l.* 18: *insert full-stop after:* dead man.

page 85, 32. 'The Caucasus mountains', *l.* 2: *change comma to full-stop after:* shouted to him.

page 93, note 17. *Insert additional note:* 'I read rationed books': A double meaning also relating to Mandelstam's strange habit of reciting the text of ration books.

NOTES

page 94, end of note 20 on 'Epigram to Stalin', *add:* Some texts have 'cockroach eyes laugh' instead of 'cockroach moustache laughs'.

The Voronezh Notebooks

POEMS 1935-1937

TRANSLATOR'S PREFACE

My first attempts to translate Osip Mandelstam started in the sixties, when I was an undergraduate at Oxford, and continued again on and off through the seventies. Although I loved to read Mandelstam's later poetry in Russian, my attempts at translation on my own didn't quite make sense as English poems. It wasn't until I teamed up with Elizabeth McKane in Princeton, and we worked together on the first draft translations of *The Moscow Notebooks*, that some of the problems in translation were resolved. Late Mandelstam is very difficult even in the original Russian. His technique of composing by mouthing words with his lips, as opposed to sitting at a table with pen and paper, gives the poems a distinctive sound quality, and a unique voice, ranging from the colloquial to the elegiac. Not only do Mandelstam's poems rhyme, but also sounds and roots evoke other sounds and roots. Form and content unite in an unsplittable whole in the Russian. So our interpretative capacities were tested to the full in trying to render meaningful poems in English.

The Moscow Notebooks were published by Bloodaxe Books in 1991, and *The Voronezh Notebooks* seemed a natural sequel to both us and the publisher. But *The Voronezh Notebooks* are, if anything, even more complex and impenetrable.

It wasn't until the Glasnost years that there was full publication of Mandelstam's poetry for the first time in Russia, as well as the publication of his widow, Nadezhda Mandelstam's, *Hope Against Hope* and *Hope Abandoned*, which had come out in the West more than fifteen years before in Russian then swiftly in Max Hayward's translation. These English titles were suggested by Nadezhda [her first name means Hope] Mandelstam herself. *Hope Against Hope* is indeed the companion book to *The Voronezh Notebooks*, covering, as it does, the Mandelstams' exile in Voronezh.

By the time of the centenary of his birth in 1991, a flurry of in-depth articles appeared. A Mandelstam Society was formed, and there was an international conference on Mandelstam held at the School of Slavonic and Eastern European Studies in London, whose papers have been recently published (Hermitage, USA, 1994). There was a further Mandelstam conference in 1994 in Voronezh.

In November 1933 Mandelstam had composed 'The Stalin Epigram', 'We are alive but no longer feel' (no. 20 in *The Second Moscow Notebook*). This, and his reading it to over a dozen people, was his death warrant and it was only a matter of time for Stalin to have him sent to certain death in the camps.

In his Introduction Victor Krivulin implies that Voronezh was a soft option for Mandelstam, and, of course, it was. But in reality the Mandelstams lived in dire poverty for most of their exile. Mandelstam was also starved of readers, a glowing exception being the young schoolteacher Natasha Shtempel, with whom he could discuss his poetry. He even resorted on one occasion to reading his latest poems on the phone to his NKVD (forerunner of the KGB) surveillance person. Mandelstam probably never really recovered from his interrogations in the Lubyanka. Nadezhda Mandelstam was allowed to accompany him into exile first to Cherdyn in the Urals and then back (within a month) to Moscow and on to Voronezh, approximately three hundred miles to the south-east of Moscow, which Mandelstam chose for his exile in the system of '–12' – any city outside the twelve major cities in Russia. His poetry was extremely demanding on him mentally. When Nadezhda was away from him or went to Moscow, on usually abortive missions to find translation work, he would become physically short of breath. He had tried to commit suicide twice: once by slashing his wrists with a razor blade that he had concealed in his boot in the Lubyanka, and once when he had jumped from the high first floor window of the old hospital in Cherdyn when he was convinced that the secret police were coming to execute him. It follows that *The Voronezh Notebooks* are even more of a miracle than they appear to be and are indeed, to quote Anna Akhmatova out of context, Mandelstam's 'passport into immortality'. Akhmatova came to see the Mandelstams in Voronezh from the 5th to the 11th February 1936 and wrote this poem about her visit:

Voronezh
Osip Mandelstam

The town stands completely icebound.
Trees, walls, snow as though under glass.
Timidly I walk over the crystals.
The painted sledge jogs along.
In Voronezh there are crows over Peter's statue,
poplars and a verdigris dome,
eroded, in the turbulent sun-dust.
Here the slopes of the powerful earth still quake
from the victory of the Tatars at Kulikovo.
The poplars like glasses touching
will chime loudly,
as though one thousand guests were toasting
our triumph at a wedding feast.

While in the room of the exiled poet
fear and the Muse stand duty in turn
and the night is endless
and knows no dawn.

[1936]

The most eloquent description of Mandelstam's situation in Voronezh is the combination of 'fear and the Muse'. In Akhmatova's *Memoir of Mandelstam* she writes: 'It is striking that expansiveness, breadth and deep breathing appeared in the poems of Mandelstam in Voronezh itself, when he was far from free.'

Mandelstam wrote his last poem in Voronezh to Natasha Shtempel on 4th May 1937. On 16th May his three year exile to Voronezh ended and the Mandelstams returned to Moscow. At the beginning of June, having been denied the right to live in Moscow they went to Savelovo, on the Volga. Here Mandelstam wrote a few poems, some of which have survived. That summer they visited Moscow often, and in the autumn they had a two week trip to Leningrad both to see Akhmatova and to try and raise some money from old friends. Afterwards they moved to Kalinin, where they lived from 17 November 1937 to 10th March 1938. They made one last trip to Leningrad in February 1938, to find that more friends had been arrested, or were too frightened to see them. In March the Literary Foundation arranged for a stay for them in the sanatorium in Samatikha, halfway between Moscow and Murom. On 3rd May Osip Mandelstam was arrested and driven away in a lorry. The formidable researcher of the KGB archives, Vitaly Shentalinsky – see *The case against Mandelstam, poet* [translated by Richard McKane] *Index on Censorship*, August/September 1991, now in book form in *The KGB's Literary Archive* by Vitaly Shentalinsky abridged and translated by John Crowfoot (Harvill) – has pieced together the interrogations of Mandelstam in 1934 and 1938. Mandelstam was sentenced to five years in a labour camp. Shentalinsky's conclusion as to the date of Mandelstam's death is the same as that of Nadezhda Mandelstam: 27th December 1938, of heart failure, in a transit camp on the way to Vladivostok. The last poem attributed to him by a campmate, Merkulov, is dated 1938:

Black night, claustrophobic barracks,
plump lice.

Nadezhda Mandelstam has this to say about the cult of the martyr that can surround Mandelstam: 'What would have become of Mandelstam if he had not been forced into a 'different channel'?

Being stronger than either me or Akhmatova, he would have accepted any channel, but suffering did not enrich him. It only destroyed him. He was hounded and stifled in every possible way, and the camp was merely the logical culmination of all he had been made to endure through the years. In effect, he was cut off before he had come to maturity – he was a slow developer – and he was still in the process of reaching it. His voice came through not because he was being hounded and smothered, but in spite of it... Considering the dynamic force with which he was endowed, he had no need of prison, exile and the camp as the main elements of his biography.' (*Hope Abandoned*, Chapter 27, *Stages*, Collins Harvill). Later in the same chapter Nadezhda Mandelstam says that what distinguished Mandelstam from all around him 'was not irresponsibility, but this infinite sense of joy'.

Mandelstam's letters to Nadezhda Mandelstam, now translated by Constance Link in *Osip Mandelstam: The Collected Prose and Letters* (Collins Harvill), show his great love and tenderness for Nadezhda. The three years that they had together in Voronezh were lived in Mandelstam's poetry. Mandelstam went far beyond being a victim, or a survivor in perilous health. In Voronezh, living in provincial isolation, he summoned a phenomenal concentration in order to transcend his circumstances, entering the most fertile phase of his poetry. Certainly he sensed joy, but he also sensed tragedy, and the cathartic effect of *The Voronezh Notebooks* reaches its height with the last poem in the book:

> The steps you once took, you won't be able to take.
> Flowers are immortal. Heaven is integral.
> What will be is only a promise.

RICHARD McKANE

INTRODUCTION

Osip Mandelstam's last and loftiest flight of poetry was preceded by the deepest abyss: a sudden personal catastrophe, which traumatised and distorted the poet's whole existence. His arrest, in May 1934, was followed by weeks of indescribable, increasing terror, and almost complete subordination to an alien and lethal will (Arthur Koestler accurately describes the plight of Stalin's victims under investigation as '*blinding darkness*'). We will probably never know what was done to Mandelstam in the torture chambers of the Lubyanka. In the four year interval between this first arrest and the last in the spring of 1938 he never spoke a word about what he endured in the Lubyanka prison. His wife had difficulty recognising the man who was brought by his guards straight from his prison cell to the platform of the Kazan station, thence to be transported to the depths of the Urals. Mandelstam seemed to have been crushed for ever by what happened to him. Emma Gerstein, a close acquaintance of the Mandelstams, remembers seeing him some time after his release [in Moscow when he had returned from Cherdyn – Tr.], when he had sort of 'got back to himself ': 'Osip was in a numbed state. His eyes were glassy. His eyelids were inflamed, and this condition never went away (most likely this was as a result of the "conveyor-belt" interrogations, which continued without a break for several days, with investigators working shifts), his eyelashes had fallen out. His arm was in a sling.'

The numbness did not pass, neither in the first months of life in exile in Cherdyn, nor in Voronezh. The shadow of 'blinding darkness' did not disappear. The blurring of his consciousness returned again and again, however hard he fought against it, either by attempting with one jerk to close his account with life by jumping out of the window in the hospital in Cherdyn, or by falling, to defend himself, into cataleptic indifference to all around him. Nevertheless, Stalin's reprisal against Mandelstam seemed to be inexplicably mild to many of his contemporaries. Exile was not considered to be so bad especially as the reason for arrest was the destructive moral-political caricature of the 'father of the peoples', contained in the poem 'We are alive but no longer feel the land under our feet' ['The Stalin Epigram', *The Second Moscow Notebook* No. 20 – Tr.]. The camps or capital punishment were threatened for much more innocent transgressions. Mandelstam was given the possibility of choosing his place of exile.

Why, after spending a short time in Cherdyn, did he choose Voronezh? It cannot be ruled out that the mentally broken poet found an argument for the place in the sound of the name – *Vorónezh*. In it could be divined the echoes of a robber's (*vorovskoy*) or rather stolen (*uvorovannoy*) life, the thieving raven (*voron*) and the robbers' knife (*nozh*). The malevolent attraction, contained in the sounds of this word, becomes more understandable if we remember that the vans in which the arrested were transported were called by the people 'black ravens' (*chornye vorony*) or 'little ravens' (*voronki*). The old Cossack song about the Black Raven, which flies in to take its prey – the life of the soldier – is sung by the doomed heroes of the first sound film *Chapayev*, whose action takes place in the Urals. The Urals were also the place to which Mandelstam was initially taken, under escort, from the Moscow prison. Several poems, written in Voronezh when Mandelstam had regained the ability to speak, are devoted to the film *Chapayev*. In one of his first attempts at poetic speech, after one and a half years of silence, he balances on the edge of a macabre pun, as he risks entering into a dangerous word play with the malevolent bird of fate:

> Pusti menya, otday menya, Voronezh:
> Uronish' ty menya il' provoronish',
> Ty vyronish' menya ili vernyosh' –
> Voronezh – blazh', Voronezh – voron, nozh.

I. 5   Let me go, return me, Voronezh:
        you will drop me or lose me,
        you will let me fall or give me back.
        Voronezh, you are a whim, Voronezh, you are a raven and a knife.

Behind these lines lies the well-known text of the song from *Chapayev*:

> 'Black raven...you won't get your prey...
> Black raven, I am not yours!'

So it was Voronezh. For Mandelstam, the name of a place with which his life was somehow connected, always meant more than just geographical names. Thus, the very title of his first book of poems, *Stone* (1913), implies the intensely Petersburgian character of his muse: ('petrus' is 'stone'). Consequently Voronezh, for Mandelstam, is nothing less than the living (suicidal) realisation of the concealed phonico-semantic metaphor. Mandelstam's choice was, subconsciously, one more step on the road to his sacrificial destruction. But it also represented a desperate desire to begin to live another

– although *stolen* life – and as a result to kill within him what was the cause of his sufferings. At the same time, with almost unerring historical sense, Mandelstam chose one of the most significant and fateful points on the map of Russia.

Peter the Great had planned for Voronezh to play a role at the end of the seventeenth century which was later given to Petersburg: to be a window to the outside world, the point at which continental Moscow broke through to the most important sea communications. The Russian Fleet was created in the shipyards of Voronezh, on the outlet to the sea of Azov. Azov, Petersburg, Sebastopol, Odessa were to follow – but Voronezh was to be first. (Ironically, now after the collapse of the USSR, Voronezh is once again a very important port for the new Russia.)

Voronezh in the nineteenth century and first half of the twentieth was deep in the provinces of the empire, and famous as one of the key centres of the Russian revolutionary movement. In 1879, the illegal, historic congress of the organisation, 'Land and Liberty', took place here. This gave rise to the famous 'People's Will', the summit of whose terrorist activity resulted in the assassination of the reformer tsar, Alexander the Second (the 'Liberator'). The 'People's Will' put an end to the successive strivings of the authorities to apply a European and civilising aspect to Russian government. The failure of the politics of government reform resulted in an explosion below, the revolution, and the Stalin terror. The 'People's Will' members were officially classed as heroes under Stalin. They were the forerunners of the Bolsheviks. Streets were named after them. Before the revolution, the ideals of the revolutionary terrorists were alien to Mandelstam. And after the revolution, he was sickened by the official exaltation of the 'People's Will'. But in the last years of his life, especially in the Voronezh period, as witnessed in the memoirs of his widow, he felt an unexpected and growing sympathy for those people, who looked on their own (and unfortunately others') lives, as just a sacrifice for the liberation and happiness of the Russian peasant. His own fate seemed now to be bound in the context of a traditional dialogue between earth and power, earth and revolution (the earth that is overturned by the ploughshare). The Russian black earth which opened up to him preserved the memory of the merciless and uncompromising 'defenders of the people', who saw in the peasant 'obshchina' (commune) not broken up into individuals, the model for the future Russian state system. In accord with the cosmic chorus, *their earth* lay in front of Mandelstam: 'The damp clods of earth of my *land and liberty*...forming a chorus' (I. 2).

In the sixties Nadezhda Mandelstam recounted this story to me. At the beginning of the thirties, Stalin visited an exhibition celebrating the 50th anniversary of the 'People's Will'. As he entered the hall, the 'heir of the revolutionary tradition' froze before two big portraits of Sofia Perovskaya and Zhelyabov, who were executed for organising the assassination of the Tsar. The portraits depicted the terrorists in the same manner as the traditional old Russian saints and hermits – with ascetic faces and huge, stern piercing eyes. They seemed to judge the descendants with the same mercilessness with which they had sentenced to death the Tsar who was, in their opinion, insufficiently devoted to the idea of democratic reforms. Stalin could not endure their look. As the all-powerful dictator's face changed, he abruptly turned and hurried out of the hall. When Mandelstam was told this story he was not surprised: he did not expect any other reaction from the tyrant.

But let us return to Voronezh in the thirties. In the exiled poet's eyes the town appeared as a miracle – as the crumbly, risen dry land, pretending to be the stormy sea. But this earth was only, after all, imitating the element of the sea, which Mandelstam missed in Voronezh. 'Oh for an inch of blue sea, for just enough to go through the eye of a needle' (I. 12), he exclaims, longing for the Mediterranean, Levantine cradle of European civilisation, from which he was now tragically torn away. Instead, before him was a chaotic deposit of poor, small houses, wildly scattered over the ravines and hillsides. The town seemed to have been forced out into the open by some inhuman power, under the sky with its Michelangelo strength, from layers of rich, fertile soil. Voronezh served, and serves, as the best illustration of the idea that the earth has absolute power over man. It is not by chance that the revolutionary agrarians, who considered the land question to be the key one for the future of Russia, once came together here, where the earth, shamelessly bare, soars up under the clouds in a burst of Titanic, creative nakedness. As for the populists, in the same way, it was here, in Voronezh, that Mandelstam, for the first time in his life, came face to face with Russia's depths, with a province that lived under the power of the earth, that is, by completely different laws from those of the more or less Europeanised Petersburg and Moscow.

Life in Voronezh, in the slums, in wretched rented flats, without money, without the right to 'intellectual' work, did not at first bring about a feeling of freedom – although the power of the interrogator and executioner over the soul of the poet gave way to another force: the power of the earth. The earth is either silent, or else it expresses itself clumsily, incoherently. It finds coherent speech only when it falls into the 'zones of culture'; space which is at home with the word. In order to start speaking again, Mandelstam had – as if to die – to become for a certain time a part of that earth without language, but overflowing with the insensible energies of speech. This is how they bring back to life the slain hero in Russian folk tales: by pouring over him first *dead* and, only after, *living* water. It was evidently precisely this second death, the death of language that Mandelstam had in mind when he wrote

I. 4   I must live, although I have died twice over,
        and flooding has driven the town half out of its mind...

It was with this poem that Mandelstam broke his year and a half of silence. His silence was broken when he felt his own integrity and rediscovered his own essence. This happened at the moment when the inert force of the earth gushed together with the force of art which was alien to these places. On 5th April 1935, Mandelstam was at a concert of the young violinist Galina Barinova, who was in Voronezh on a concert tour. From that day on it was as if he was born again. From that day he began to write poems.

The Russian writer from the end of the last century, Gleb Uspensky, who was close to the 'People's Will', has a story. In *She Put Me Straight*, a young teacher, Tyapushkin, is abandoned in a Russian village in the depths of the provinces. He comes up against the monstrous wildness of the everyday life that surrounds him. He grows dull and sinks and starts to drink too much. The earth seems to devour and digest him. But suddenly in the middle of a drunken fever, he remembers with unusual clarity how once in Paris, in the Louvre, he saw an inhumanly beautiful ancient sculpture, the Venus de Milo. This memory returns him to his humanity. The hero is reborn to a new life: Venus has put him straight.

But in contrast to Uspensky's hero, Mandelstam was not young, his psychological and physical strength was on the wane, and the bursts of creative energy were destructive for his physical existence. But convulsively and without looking back, although with a certain inner sense of doom, he gave himself up to the element of art. In two years in Voronezh he noted down ninety poems (not counting the huge number of transitory variants and rough drafts), that is more than a third of all the lyric texts he composed.

S.B. Rudakov, the exiled Leningrad poet, the involuntary Ecker-man [Goethe's literary secretary – Tr.] to Mandelstam, who was the main person Mandelstam talked and listened to in Voronezh and who was the witness of the debilitating and self-destructive process of creating words (and to whom 'Black Earth' is dedicated, one of the best Voronezh poems) wrote in his diary for spring 1935: 'Mandelstam is in a frenzy of work. I have never seen anything like it...I am beholding a working machine (or perhaps it's more accurate to say organism) of poetry. There's no man left: it's Michelangelo. He sees and remembers nothing. He walks around and mutters: "a black fern in a green night". For four lines he pronounces four hundred. I mean this absolutely literally. He sees nothing. He doesn't remember his lines. He repeats over and over, and detaches the repetition and writes something new...' Rudakov often notes in his diary the most striking phrases of Mandelstam, and among them, the surprising confession of what Voronezh gave to the author of *Stone* and *Tristia*: Mandelstam affirmed that he 'was forced all his life to write *prepared* pieces, but Voronezh brought, perhaps for the first time, an open newness and straightness...' (He was put straight!)

All in all the Voronezh poems do present an open system. Despite giving the impression of external chaos and the self-sufficiency of separate fragments of poems, and despite, at first glance, the fragmentation and ellipsis, they do create a unique example of integral, artistic unity. Unlike classical works, they are based not on symmetry and contrapuntal parts, not on the sequential development of the subject, but on the principles of an organic, synchronic development of several semantic (both musical and phonic) motifs and themes, which move ahead simultaneously in different semantic and emotional tonalities. These poems are grouped together in three extensive cycles, which form the so-called *Voronezh Notebooks*. The *First Voronezh Notebook* contains twenty-two poems, composed from April to August 1935. The *Second*, the most expansive, brings together more than forty texts, written down at the end of 1936 and beginning of 1937 (from 6th December to the end of February). The last, the *Third* (March to beginning of May 1937), is similar in quantity to the *First*, also having twenty-two poems.

In each notebook, one can single out typical centres or knots of sense, texts or groups of texts, in which the basic motifs are condensed and come together. But the less significant, "transitional", seemingly chance poems also play an essential part. Outside the cycle, they give the impression of being rough draft variants, however, within each notebook they create a vital speech background, a definite sense-forming sound, the plasma of speech, from which the best works of the Voronezh period are born. In such a way, the process of making and of the birth of poetic speech moves to the fore. The context and emotional range of expression is broadened very precisely because of the 'chance' fragments, which frequently lower the generally high, tragic tonality of the Voronezh poems. It is enough, for example, to compare one of Mandelstam's most intense poems, 'Buried in the lion's den' (II. 45), where the poet sees himself as the prophet Daniel, cast into the fiery abyss and the deadly *pit*, and an extempore poem which makes absolutely no sense outside the general context, and which contains a joking self-characterisation of the poet.

I. 8   There was little of the straight line in him,
        his morals were not lily-white
        and so this street,
        or rather this pit,
        is named after
        this Mandelstam.

This comparison makes it obvious how important to Mandelstam is the principle of complementariness, and how strong are the intricate and not always graspable intertextual connections.

Perhaps Mandelstam chooses compositional fracture and fragmentation precisely because he is creating within the limits of a certain macrotext, in the frame of something created and mastered before him, warmed by the alien breath of artistic space. There are 'prepared' pieces already existent in the world and they are a real force. The majority of the Voronezh poems in one way or another touch on the theme of high art, of European culture, perceived by Mandelstam as a homogeneous, integral education. In Voronezh he misses this ideal Europe, whether it is Hungary or Poland, Italy of the renaissance, or France of the Barbisons, the Germany of Bach, or ancient Greece, or even his own Petersburg, whose winter landscapes time and again arise in the Voronezh poems. But at the same time, for him, this world is completed, concluded, and in some sense a province of shadows, like the West was for the ancient Egyptians. It is a book which has already been written, on top of which he writes his text, bringing in fleeting and chance impressions of today to the first forms of European culture. The main thing for him is the process of writing itself, the creative and ethical sense of working with speech.

However 'writing' is not the right word to apply to the late Mandelstam. In Voronezh he does not '*write*', but literally speaks out, screams out, and voices his poems. The main part of the Voronezh texts are handwritten by his wife to his dictation, occasionally inconsistent and assuming mutually exclusive variants in the reading. It is all in the voice, in the movement, in the plasmic fusion of the speech, which excludes the linear logic which exists in the language system. The poet often does not separate one piece from another: whole chunks of poems migrate from one poem to another, almost without textual changes, but with this they change till they are unrecognisable, to a polarised change of senses, in dependence on the new context. Mandelstam spoke out his poems away from home, outside the walls 'in the air', throwing his head back high and ridiculously proudly, and rushing headlong along the winding, crooked little streets of Voronezh. Once and once only, he made an attempt to write 'like other people', at a writing table, when, moved by either extreme desperation, or captivated by an entirely new artistic problem, he composed the 'Ode to Stalin', which bewildered not only his contemporaries but also future generations. But it cannot be ruled out that the feeling of the genre in the first place fixed the poet to his table: the 'state' plastic art of the ode somehow denied the rushing about of the author along the dull backstreets of the terrified Soviet provincial town.

The poet Osip Mandelstam in Voronezh – as represented in the stories of eye-witnesses, who were distant from poetry, but who remembered well that wild figure on the streets of their home town – is very reminiscent of the composer Johannes Brahms in the perception of the rather simple Hungarian peasants, who watched in amazement and fear as the strange musician rushed aimlessly, and for days on end, round the surrounding fields and meadows, muttering various things, singing and whistling, now imitating the birds, and then collapsing with exhaustion from the abundance of the overflowing element of music and the initial creative chaos which had not yet found a clear form. Mandelstam was also like the town madman, and the Voronezh street kids teased him almost to his face. His street nickname among the local hooligans was *general*, which in a remarkable way combines both the nuance of an instinctive respect which the simple Russian folk have for madmen with 'education', and, on the border of denunciation, the merciless, social description of the poet as an *outsider*, as a class enemy (in the context of the thirties the word 'general' was never applied to Soviet commanders, but referred only to 'former people', to the Whites and to those from before the Soviet regime).

Mandelstam himself felt that he was a bird, a singing bird: a bird in a cage. Even the intoxicating, spring air of Voronezh was a cage. The poet's own body was not able to bear the mental freedom which opened out to him when he found his voice again. This bird-like, fragile freedom, which is possible only in childhood, made Mandelstam remember those days when the world was first revealed to him:

> A childish mouth chews its chaff,
> and smiles as it chews.
> Like a dandy I'll throw back my head
> and see the goldfinch.
>
> (II. 4, *variant*)

'Chaff in the mouth' is none other than the still incoherent first words to be pronounced. The words are uniquely genuine, their own, because they have not acquired the aftertaste of an outsider's hostile speech. 'An outsider's speech' is also a cage, a lie, a fiction, slander (in the historical context of the epoch of the Great Terror, the word 'slander' figured in each political trial, and the accusation of 'slander against the Soviet system' was levelled at Mandelstam himself when he was arrested). But, according to Mandelstam, there is one unique, genuine source of 'slander': the cage itself, that is the forcibly legalised system of false values:

> II. 5 The cage is a hundred bars of lies
> the perch and the little plank are slanderous.
> Everything in the world is inside out...

In a world turned inside-out for Mandelstam it is speech, not language as a 'prepared' system, which is the last reality – precisely speech, in its organic unbrokendownness, producing an 'individual formula of breathing' which, like fingerprints, is unrepeatable and unique to each person. Articulating his own 'formula for breathing', the poet speaks for others: the voiceless, the nameless, the unknown, who remain a pure and unrealised potential of speech (as in the prophetic 'Poem to the Unknown Soldier'). He raises speech to the condition of Language. One can take away language from the poet, one can force the whole country to speak in an artificial, ideologised, Soviet 'new-speak', but the authorities are powerless to take away the living breath from human lips:

> I. 14 Having deprived me of seas, of running and flying away,
> and allowing me only to walk upon the violent earth,
> what have you achieved? A splendid result:
> you could not stop my lips from moving.

There is a serious temptation (the basis for which is presented not so much in the poems as in the biography, and Mandelstam's tragic end) to see in the poet a consistent and conscientious fighter against the totalitarian regime, or, at least, the victim of his own liberal humanistic, 'westerniser' aspirations. Many of those who genuinely love Mandelstam and have a subtle understanding of his poetry, would prefer that such texts as 'Stanzas' (I. 11) and the 'Ode to Stalin' did not exist among his creative heritage. These poems are perceived now, in the context of a new epoch, as manifestations of a momentary weakness on the part of the poet, as born of fear and of an understandable wish, in human terms, to adapt himself to the existent, though monstrous and debasing, order of things. Even Academician S.S. Averintsev, the venerable culturologist and expert on poetry and the author of an extensive critical and biographical study on Mandelstam, is convinced that 'work on "The Ode" could not but be a darkening of his mind and self-destructive to his genius'. He does not mention 'Stanzas' at all, although it is one of the key poems of the Voronezh period. On the other hand, the former Stalinists in the seventies and eighties eagerly turned to the 'loyal' poems of Mandelstam, seeing in them the possibility of demonstrating the power of the ideas of Bolshevism, which were capable of 'reshoeing' (a political term of the thirties, which referred mainly to changing the intelligentsia, the peasantry and criminal world) even such an inveterate enemy of the Soviet authorities as 'the singer of the grand bourgeoisie', Osip Mandelstam. Thus, A. Dymshits, an important party official on literary matters, in his foreword to the first posthumous edition of Mandelstam's poems in his own country (1973) convinces the reader that the poet after a long period of vacillation nevertheless realised he was wrong in his argument with the 'new life', and only an unfortunate accident (his death in the concentration camp [though Dymshits does not mention this – Tr.]) got in the way of his joining the amenable chorus of Soviet poets praising the 'socialist fatherland'. The critic cites examples, eloquent enough in his opinion, of the 'reshod and Sovietised' Mandelstam, such as:

I. 11 (II)   I love the Red Army greatcoat and its folds...

or:

I. 10 (III)   and I would have liked to have kept
              this mad calm land safe in a greatcoat.

or:

I. 11 (III)   I must live, breathing, *growing big and Bolshevik* (my italics – V.K.)

or:

I. 11 (I)   rather to go into the world as a landowning peasant
              enters the collective farm – and the people are good...

However, if one returns these lines to the context from which they have been torn, their lack of a single meaning becomes at least obvious, and their other meanings are not grasped by the literary ideologue. One has to bear in mind that Mandelstam's poems of the thirties are unusually full of political terminology. The pressure of propaganda from the pages of magazines and books, the radio, and at the numerous meetings, drumming every day into the heads of the people a quite limited set of sociological concepts – all this could not but be felt by the poet. One could block one's ears and close one's eyes, but Mandelstam, in principle, was tormentingly open to outside impressions. The ideologemes that prevailed around him were involuntarily drawn into his work on speech, and he used them as natural material, supplied by life itself, for the realisation of other purely aesthetic aims, absolutely not envisaged by the State creators of the ideological language. He washes away the definition and forced single-meaningness of the concepts central to Soviet ideology, and places them in exotic language surroundings, decomposing their sense from within so that he may include them in the semantic and associative ranks which belong to his poetic speech system alone. He considers them in the context of Russian classical and – broader – world culture, at the same time destroying their claims to spiritual rule by subordinating them to more universal laws and norms.

As an illustration of this process, one can turn to any of the examples proffered by Dymshits. For instance behind the line 'I love the Red Army greatcoat and its folds...' (I.11 (II)) there is a complex extra-textual metaphor that refers the reader back to the anthologised poem of Tyutchev (1803-73): 'I love the storm at the start of May...' In Mandelstam's 'Stanzas' from which the quotation above is taken, the Red Army greatcoat is actually compared with a storm cloud. 'Stanzas', which was composed in May 1935, describes the May Day parade, contrasting thus the romantic yet terrible appearance of nature (the storm) with the malevolent, celebratory rapture of one of the central Soviet festivals. This metaphor can be broadened further if we remember that the very title 'Stanzas' is also a classic title and refers us back to Pushkin (1799-1837), whose poem 'Stanzas' (1827) presented a flattering parallel for the ruling tsar Nicholas the First (1794-1855) with Peter the Great (1672-1725), and which for a long time served as the most brilliant example of loyal, monarchist lyric poetry. The liberal-minded public turned away from Pushkin after the publication of 'Stanzas'.

In comparing his fate with that of Pushkin, Mandelstam in fact poses the question of the right of the poet to evaluate the state not as an empirical, political reality, but as an aesthetic category, capable of eliciting the same rapture the grandness of Rome did for its admirers. But the development of the extra-textual metaphor goes further. The author of the first 'Stanzas', who had aestheticised the pomp and power of the empire created by Peter the First, and destroyed by the Bolsheviks one hundred years later, is turned into the main poet of the Bolsheviks and is canonised in the same way as the terrorist members of the People's Will. His world of poetry was transferred into an alien historical context, and in that context the most malevolent things were the splendid jubilee celebrations held throughout the country (January 1937). The centenary of Pushkin's death, was celebrated against a background of the bloody slaughterhouse working at full power at the height of the Great Terror, and the jubilee commission, apart from academics and writers, was comprised of the real executioners, the generals of the NKVD and party bosses.

In *The Voronezh Notebooks*, 'Stanzas' is followed by the poem 'The day was five-headed...' (I. 12), where there is a direct mention by name of Pushkin, who had been appropriated by the Bolsheviks. One of the guards who was accompanying the exiled Mandelstam to the Urals, according to Nadezhda Mandelstam's memoirs, continuously read from a small volume of the great Russian poet; he was indignant at how cruelly the tsar's government persecuted the freedom-loving genius, not even understanding how absurd and blackly comical was his – as gaoler of another, living, great poet – genuine sympathy for the sufferings of the author of 'Poltava', 'The Bronze Horseman' and, of course, 'Stanzas'. The tracks of this strange meeting of Mandelstam with Pushkin are in the lines:

> So that the wondrous goods of Pushkin should not fall into the hands
>   of parasites,
> a generation of Pushkin scholars learn to read and write in overcoats
>   with revolvers...

And was it not that meeting that jolted Mandelstam to compose his 'Stanzas', and forced him to look, as though from the side, at himself and at those liberal values which before his arrest and exile had seemed to him to be unshakable? We can only guess about this.

Even native, experienced experts in the Russian language cannot always read Mandelstam adequately. We can often only guess at the depth of his poems, the scale and ramifications of his associative moves. We can only contemplate the general contours of the grand and enigmatic composition of his poetry, the greater part of which is concealed by a thick mist. But the feeling of heaviness of the subject matter, and the density of the verbal material, convince us that before us is not a void, nor fiction, but reality. A time comes when the veil of mist disperses, and many of the insights of the poet, which seemed crazy and vague, are realised in the historical road of Russia itself. As far as *The Voronezh Notebooks* are concerned, they will remain not simply actual and urgent, but behind them can be seen a new, unread page of Russian and perhaps even European history.

VICTOR KRIVULIN
St Petersburg, 1993
(translated by Richard McKane)

RECOGNISING MANDELSTAM

There are few poets who can accompany and thrill readers or indeed translators throughout their lives. Key poems resonate at different stages of one's life: 'recognition' or 'recognising' as Osip Mandelstam said in the early poem 'Tristia' is paramount to life and poetry and has much to do with memory. Translation gains a poet recognition in another language. This inevitably involves re-reading. I reread Mandelstam – he is an old Russian and English friend I recognise. If this book tempts any reader to learn Russian I would be happy for the music of Russian poetry is difficult to capture in English, whereas there have been great successes in "formal" translation from English and other poetries into Russian which has a great wealth of rhymes (although there are many gaps to be filled in modern English poetry in Russian).

Elizabeth and I – working lovingly a decade ago – concentrated on transferring the content, the rhythm of the images rather than attempting to reproduce rhyme or Russian rhythm/metre schemes (both of which have heavily influenced my own poetry). Rhyming words do not translate directly, though I am indebted to my old Russian teacher Richard Pollock for the exceptional pun: *'uchitel'/muchitel'*: mentor/ tormentor. If Mandelstam's rhyme and rhythm scheme in their quantity and quality in English are 'unrecognisable', we still hope that the specific gravity of individual poems is preserved and that these two books together form the body of Mandelstam's later poetry. We have made a few significant revisions in this new edition.

I think there was a tendency up till Glasnost when Mandelstam exploded on the Russian readership – in print runs totalling over a million – to concentrate on the later Mandelstam as the persecuted poet of terror. Reading the poems challenges the exclusivity of this myth. The changing times gave back Mandelstam to his countrymen after non-publication or partial publication for over forty or fifty years. His poems are more often than not jubilant actions uncovering the zest in life and world poetry against the grain of Soviet everyday life. As he says in his prose, they were stolen air. But to use modern terminology he is fundamentally and mentally anti-terror: this is why he tackles the tyrant Stalin, who is the opposite pole of himself, in his poems. This is his challenge to history and indeed philosophy, but it is only part of his poetry.

It is with deep sadness that I have to add that our friend, the poet Victor Krivulin, died in March 2001 at the age of 56. We reprint his Introductions without alteration. Krivulin did not put Mandelstam on a pedestal, but contextualises him as a poet of his age and above the age. Yet in saying defiantly 'No, never was I anyone's contemporary' in a poem written in 1924, the time of Lenin's death, Mandelstam is stretching out beyond the terror and horror as he did in this quatrain from the 'Ode to Stalin':

> Heaped hills of human heads go off into the distance.
> I grow smaller there, they won't notice me any more;
> but in much loved books and children's games
> I shall arise to say that the sun is shining.

RICHARD McKANE
London, 2003

FIRST
VORONEZH
NOTEBOOK

1. 'Black candle'

It is your fate, for your narrow shoulders to turn red under the lashes,
red under the lashes, to burn in the frost,

for your childish hands to lift the iron,
to lift the iron and tie bundles,

for your tender bare feet to tread on glass,
to tread on glass and on the bloody sand.

And as for me, I burn after you like a black candle,
burn like a black candle and dare not pray.

[February 1934]

2. Black Earth

The damp clods of earth of my land and liberty
are all overworked, extra black and well-groomed.
They are all in airy little well-tended ridges,
crumbling, and forming a chorus.
In the early spring the earth is bluish black,
and ploughing is pacifist work.
The rumour is ploughed open revealing a thousand mounds.
Know this, there is something boundless within these boundaries.

The earth is a mistake and a rifle butt,
immovable, however often you implore her on bended knee.
She sharpens our hearing with a decaying flute.
She freezes our ears with a morning clarinet.

The fat crust of the earth is so pleasant against the ploughshare
as the steppe lies in the April upheaval.
Salutations, black earth, be strong and alert,
there's a fertile black silence in work.

[April 1935]

122

3. 'In strangers' homes'

I live overlooking choice back-gardens –
where Ivan the watchman could wander.
The wind works for free in the factories.
The log path across the marsh runs into the distance.

The black ploughed night of the steppe borders
has frozen into tiny bead fires.
Behind the wall the crotchety landlord stomps
around in his Russian boots.

The floorboards are splendidly crooked,
they are the coffin-boards of this deck.
I sleep badly in strangers' homes,
and my own life is not near me.

[April 1935]

4. 'I must live'

I must live, although I have died twice over,
and flooding has driven the town half out of its mind.
See how good it looks, the happy, prominent,
fat crust of the earth so pleasant against the ploughshare.
The steppe lies in the April upheaval –
and the sky, the sky is your Michelangelo.

[April 1935]

5. 'Voronezh'

Let me go, return me, Voronezh:
you will drop me or lose me,
you will let me fall or give me back.
Voronezh, you are a whim, Voronezh, you are a raven and a knife.

[April 1935]

6. 'My earphones'

My earphones, my little informers,
I will remember those short, sweet Voronezh nights:
a voice not yet drunk to the dregs of French champagne
and the sirens from Red Square at midnight...

How's the metro? Be quiet, keep it to yourself,
don't ask if the buds are bursting...
The chimes of the Kremlin clocks
are the language of space compressed to a dot.

[April 1935]

7. 'Red Square'

Yes, I'm lying in the earth, my lips are moving,
and what I say, every schoolboy will learn by heart:
in Red Square, the earth curves more sharply than anywhere else,
and the slope is repaired by 'volunteer' labour.

The earth curves more sharply than anywhere else in Red Square,
and its slope is unexpectedly expansive,
rolling down to the rice fields
for as long as the last slave on earth is alive.

[May 1935]

8. 'Mandelstam Street'

What street is this?
Mandelstam Street.
What a devil of a name!
However you turn it
it sounds crooked, not straight.

There was little of the straight line in him,
his morals were not lily-white
and so this street,
or rather this pit,
is named after
this Mandelstam.

[April 1935]

9. Children at the Barber's

We're still full of life to the highest degree.
Dresses and blouses of butterfly
palmate Chinese cotton still flit around
in the cities of the Soviet Union.

The clippers are set at the closest cut
and still collect their chestnut bribes,
and the reasonable, thick locks
fall on the clean cloth napkins.

There are still plenty of martlets and swallows.
The comet has not yet given us the plague,
and the sensible purple inks
write with tails that carry stars.

[24 May 1935]

10. 'The Kama'

I

The eye darkens as the towns kneel on stilts of oak
beside the Kama river.

The burning fir grove, disguised and bearded
in spiders' webs becomes young again as it runs into the water.

The water was bumped against one hundred and four paddles,
and carried us up and down to and from Kazan and Cherdyn.

Thus I sailed down the river with drawn curtains at the window,
with curtains drawn at the window and a blazing head.

My wife stayed awake with me for five nights,
stayed awake for five nights as she coped with the three guards.

II

The eye darkens as the towns kneel on stilts of oak
beside the Kama river.

The burning fir grove, disguised and bearded
in spiders' webs becomes young again as it runs into the water.

The water was bumped against one hundred and four paddles,
and carried us up and down to and from Kazan and Cherdyn.

The timber, piled with the rabble, burnt with the shrubs,
collapsed like the sound of machine gun fire.

They're shouting on the 'Tobol' ferry. The 'Ob' is beside the raft.
The river miles mounted up.

III

As I went away I looked at the coniferous east –
the flooding Kama rushed at the buoys.

I would have liked to have ridged the hill with a bonfire,
but you'd scarcely have time to preserve a forest.

I would have liked to have settled here – do you understand? –
in the venerable Urals where people live,

and I would have liked to have kept
this mad, calm land safe in a greatcoat.

[April – May 1935]

11. Stanzas

I

I do not want to squander
the last penny of my soul among youths bred in a hothouse,
rather to go into the world as a landowning peasant
enters the collective farm – and the people are good.

II

I love the Red Army greatcoat and its folds,
stretching to the heels, simple and smooth sleeves.
Its cut is like a black cloud over the Volga.
Hanging full at the back and the chest,
so that nothing wasted
it can get rolled up in summer.

III

A damned stitch, a ridiculous enterprise
separated us. And now understand this,
I must live, breathing, growing big and Bolshevik,
and before death I must become better-looking
and still be around to play with people a little.

IV

Imagine how I rushed around
in a twelve inch commotion, in dear old Cherdyn
among the funnel smoke from the Ob and Tobol,
and the grub and the spittle and lies and everything,
like a cock in the transparent summer darkness.
I did not watch to the end the battles of slanderous dominoes,
shrugging off the tapping of the informing woodpecker,
I jumped into my mind.

V

And you, Moscow, my sister, are so light,
when you meet your brother's plane
before the first tram bell –
you are more tender than the sea, a tossed salad
of wood, glass and milk.

VI

My country spoke with me,
spoiled, and scolded me, and did not read me;
but when I was grown up, as a witness
it all at once noticed me, and suddenly like a lens
set me on fire with a beam from the Admiralty.

VII

I must live, breathing, growing big and Bolshevik,
working with speech, not listening to my inner ear, with my
            companion.
I hear the thudding of Soviet machines in the Arctic.
I remember everything, the necks of German brothers,
and that man who was both gardener and executioner who filled
his leisure time with the lilac comb of the Lorelei.

VIII

I am not robbed, and I am not wretched,
just completely overwhelmed.
My string is taut as in *The Song of Igor*.
After asphyxiation
you hear in my voice the dry dampness
of the black earth acres – my last weapon.

[May-June 1935]

12. 'The day was five-headed'

The day was five-headed. For five consecutive days
I shrank, proud of space because it rose on yeast.
Dreaming was greater than hearing, hearing was older than dreaming,
    blended together, sensitised...
And the high roads chased us with coach horses.

The day was five-headed, and driven mad from the dance,
the horsemen rode and the unmounted walked, a mass of black:
as the white nights dilated the aorta of power, the knife blades
turned the eye into coniferous flesh.

Oh for an inch of blue sea, for just enough to go through the eye of a
    needle,
so that the pair of us escorted by time could be carried well under
    sail.
This is a Russian tale of dry-mint and wooden spoons.
Where are you, three fine fellows from the iron gates of the GPU?

So that the wondrous goods of Pushkin should not fall into the
    hands of parasites,
a generation of Pushkin scholars learn to read and write in
    overcoats with revolvers –
the young lovers of white-toothed poems,
O for an inch of blue sea, for just enough to go through the eye
    of a needle!

The train went to the Urals. Chapayev talked and galloped
into our open mouths from off the sound picture –
and we leapt into the saddle as we drowned
in the sheet screen back behind the log huts.

[April – May 1935]

132

13. 'Chapayev'

Even fish have found a way to talk
from the damp screen.
The talking picture approached
me, you and all of us.

The officers moulded in the new regime
scoffed at the steep curve of losses,
and, clenching their deadly cigarettes between their teeth,
advanced into the gaping groin of the plain.

One could hear the low buzzing roar
of planes, burned to ash.
The admiral's cheeks were scraped
with the English horse razor.

My country, measure me, and redraw me.
The heat of the enslaved land is wonderful!
Chapayev's rifle misfired.
Help! Unleash! Divide!

[April – June 1935]

14. 'Having deprived me'

Having deprived me of seas, of running and flying away,
and allowing me only to walk upon the violent earth,
what have you achieved? A splendid result:
you could not stop my lips from moving.

[May 1935]

15. 'To praise a dead woman'

Is it possible to praise a dead woman?
She is estranged and powerful...
An alien-loving power has brought her
to a violent, hot grave.

The rigid swallows of her curved brows
flew to me from the grave
to say they had laid down to rest
in their cold Stockholm bed.

Your family were proud of your great-grandfather's violin,
and it was beautiful at the neck.
You parted your scarlet lips
in laughter, so Italian, so Russian.

I cherish your unhappy memory,
wilding, bear cub, Mignon.
But the wheels of the windmills hibernate in the snow,
and the postman's horn is frozen.

[3 June 1935 – 14 December 1936]

16. 'St Isaac's'

St Isaac's is like icicles on the eyelashes of the dead,
and the aristocratic streets are blue.
The death of the organ grinder, the she-bear's coat,
and strangers' logs in the fireplace.

Fire, a hunter, drives out
the flock of wagons, scattering them.
The earth, this furnished globe, rushes on,
and the mirror contorts the megalomaniac.

There is disorder and mist on the landings.
Breath after breath and singing.
Schubert is in his fur coat with his frozen talisman,
movement after movement after movement.

[3 June 1935]

17. 'Rome nights'

Rome nights are weighty ingots:
the emotion that attracted the young Goethe.
I'll answer for this, but I am not going to lose:
there is a life outside the law and it has many depths.

[June 1935]

18. The Violinist

They run like a throng of gipsies,
chasing after the long-fingered Paganini,
one with a Czech sneeze, another with a Polish dance,
and still another with a Hungarian refrain.

Comfort me with your playing,
proud little prodigy
whose sound is broad as the Yenisey,
little Polish girl, whose head
has a mound of curls, fit for Marina Mnishek.
My violinist, your bow is suspicious.

Comfort me with chestnut Chopin
and serious Brahms. No, stop.
Instead comfort me with powerfully wild Paris,
with the floury, sweaty carnival,
or the flighty young Vienna of home-brewed beer,

with conductors' tailcoats,
with fireworks over the Danube, with races,
and an intoxicating waltz overflowing
from the coffin into the cradle.

Play then till my aorta bursts,
play with a cat's head in your mouth.
There were three devils, now you're the fourth,
the final wonderful devil in full flower.

[5 April – July 1935]

19. 'Wave after wave'

Wave after wave runs on, breaking the wave's back,
throwing itself at the moon with a prisoner's longing.
The young janissary depths,
the unlulled capital of waves,
swerve and thrash, digging a ditch in the sand.

And in the air, ragged with the twilight,
crenellations appear in an unborn wall.
The soldiers of the suspicious sultans
fall from the foamy staircase, dispersing in spray and separating,
and cold eunuchs carry round the poison cup.

[27 June – July 1935]

20. 'I shall perform a smoky ceremony'

I shall perform a smoky ceremony:
in this opal, in this exile before me, lie
the strawberries of a summer by the sea;
the doublefrank carnelians,
and the agate of the brotherhood of ants.

But dearer to me is the simple soldier
of the deep sea – grey and wild
which pleases no one.

[July 1935]

21. 'The Airmen'

I will not return my hired dust to the earth
as a floury white butterfly.
I want the thinking body
to turn into a street, a country,
where the vertebrate, charred body
will realise its true length.

The cries of the dark green pine branches,
wreaths from the depth of the well,
draw out life and precious time,
leaning on the deathly machines –
the hoops of red-bannered firs,
the dense wreaths with their alphabet of letters.

The comrades of the last call-up were going
to work in the harsh skies,
the infantry passed by silently,
carrying exclamation marks of rifles on their shoulders.

There were anti-aircraft weapons in their thousands,
and brown or blue-eyed,
the people, people, people passing by in disarray
who will carry on for them?

[Spring-Summer 1935 – 30 May 1936]

22. 'No, it's not a migraine'

No, it's not a migraine but pass the menthol stick anyway –
neither the languishing of art, nor the beauties of joyful space...

Life began in the trough with a moist, throaty whisper,
and continued with soft kerosene smog.

Somewhere afterwards at a summer house life suddenly flared up,
no one knows why, in a woody shagreen binding like a huge
blaze of lilac.

No, it's not a migraine but pass the menthol stick anyway –
neither the languishing of art, nor the beauties of joyful space.

Further on, through the stained glass, squinting, tortured, I see
the sky threatening like a cudgel, the earth like a reddish bald
patch...

Further on, I don't remember, further it's as though everything
was broken off,
a slight smell of pitch and, it seems, of bad blubber oil...

No, it's not a migraine but the cold of genderless space,
the whistle of ripped gauze and the noise of a carbolic guitar.

[July 1935]

SECOND
VORONEZH
NOTEBOOK

1. 'Sadko'

Sadko of the factories and gardens,
whistle from behind the houses, and the forests,
a whistle longer than the goods trains,
whistle for the power of my night-time labours.

Whistle, old man, breathe sweetly,
like the Novgorod merchant Sadko,
whistle deep under the blue sea,
whistle loud and long into the depth of the ages,
the siren of Soviet towns.

[6-9 December 1936]

2. Birth of the Smile

When a child starts to smile,
with a split of bitterness and sweetness,
honestly, the ends of his smile
go off into the anarchy of the ocean.

He feels invincibly good,
the corners of his lips play in glory,
already the rainbow stitch is sewn,
for the endless understanding of reality.

At the flux and flow of the mouth's snail
the mainland arose out of the water on its paws,
and one Titanic moment is revealed
to the slender tune of praise and surprise.

[9 December 1936 – 17 January 1937]

3. 'I'll wonder at the world'

I'll wonder at the world a little longer still,
at the children and the snow.
But a smile is like the road – it can't be faked,
and is disobedient, not a slave.

[9-13 December 1936]

4. 'The Goldfinch'

My goldfinch, I'll throw back my head,
let's look at the world together:
the winter's day is prickly like chaff,
does it seem as harsh to your eyes?

Do you realise, goldfinch,
what a flash finch you are, with your little tail-feathers
like a rowboat, feathers – black and yellow,
your throat, flowing with colour.

What airy thoughts does he have in his mind?
He looks back and forth, he's on guard.
Now he's not looking, he's flown off,
a flash of black and red, yellow and white!

[10-27 December 1936]

5. 'The Cage'

When the goldfinch like rising dough
suddenly moves, as a heart throbs,
anger peppers its clever cloak
and its nightcap blackens with rage.

The cage is a hundred bars of lies
the perch and little plank are slanderous.
Everything in the world is inside out,
and there is the Salamanca forest
for disobedient, clever birds.

[after 8 December 1936]

6. 'Today is a little yellow'

Today is a little yellow round the beak,
I cannot understand it –
and the estuary opening into the sea
dotted with anchors, looks at me through the mist.

The progress of the warships is quiet,
quiet through the faded water,
and the narrow pencil boxes of canals
are even more black under the ice.

[9-28 December 1936]

7. 'I am at the heart of the age'

I am at the heart of the age – the road is unclear,
and time makes the aim distant:
the staff's tired ash tree,
and the copper's poor mould.

[14 December 1936]

8. 'They, not you nor I'

They, not you nor I,
have total control over all the endings of words.
The reed they play sings a hollow song.
The heaviness of their breath will be drawn in
with gratitude through the snails of human lips.

They are nameless. If you penetrate their cartilage,
you will be the heir of their princedoms.

And for the others with their living hearts,
wandering in their confusion and windings,
you will portray for them the ebb and flow
of their joys and torture.

[9-27 December 1936]

9. 'The Idol'

The idol is indolent inside the mountain,
in the infinite security of well-ordered chambers.
The fat of rich necklaces dripping from his neck
guards the ebb and flow of his dreams.

When he was a boy, and a peacock played with him,
they fed him on an Indian rainbow.
They gave him milk from pink earthenware bowls,
and did not spare the cochineal.

The sleep-lulled bone is knotted.
He thinks with bone and feels with his brow,
and tries desperately to remember his human appearance –
his knees, arms, shoulders become human –
he smiles with his broad smile.

[10-26 December 1936]

10. 'The master gunsmith'

The master gunsmith,
tailor of blacksmith's memorials,
will say to me: don't worry, old man,
we'll run one up for you.

[December 1936]

11. 'The family sound'

The family sound of violas and harps,
is in the law of the pine wood.
All the trunks grow twisted and naked –
but still there are harps and violas.
As though Aeolus had started
to bend each trunk into a harp
and gave up, pitying the roots
pitying the trunk, saving strength,
and roused the viola and the harp
to resound in the bark, turning brown.

[16-18 December 1936]

146

12. 'Zadonsk'

It's easy to take off the stubble of hibernation
with the thin blade of the razor.
Let's remember together
the half-Ukrainian summer.

You, distinguished tree-tops,
the feasts of shaggy trees,
occupy the place of honour in Ruisdael's pictures –
and to begin, just one bush
in the amber and meat of red clays is needed.

The earth runs uphill. It's pleasant
to look at the clear layers
and to be the landowner
of an expansive seven-chambered simplicity.

Its hills flew off, dotted with light hayricks,
into the distant future.
The steppe boulevard of its roads
is like a string of tents in the heat of the shade.
The willow rushed to the fire,
and the poplar got up proudly!
The track of frosty smoke hovers
over the yellow labour camp of stubble.

And the river Don is still like a half-breed beauty,
silvery, shallow and awkward.
Drawing half buckets of water
she would get confused, like my soul,

when the burden of the evenings
lay on hard beds,
and the trees caroused and rustled
coming out from the banks.

[15-27 December 1936]

13. 'This region is in dark water'

This region is in dark water –
muddy crops, a bucket of storms.
These are not the lands of a gentleman farmer,
but the nucleus of an ocean.
I love this region's map,
it's like Africa.
If you light it you can't count
all the transparent holes in the plywood...
Anna, Rossosh and Gremyache –
I repeat the names.
I saw the eiderdown whiteness of snows
from the carriage window.

I circled round the fields of the State farms,
my mouth was full of air,
the menacing suns of sunflowers
rotated right into the eyes.
I entered at night into the gauntleted
Tambov, splendid with snow.
I saw the Tsna – an ordinary river –
white, white, it was covered in white.
I will remember for ever
the work day of the familiar earth,
and I will never forget
the Vorobyovo district committee.

Where am I? What's wrong with me?
The winterless steppe is bare:
this is the stepmother of Koltsov –
no, you're joking, it's the motherland of the goldfinch.
Only a review of a dumb city,
with icy ground,
only the teapot talking
to itself at night,
and the trains calling each other
in the dregs of the steppe air,
and the Ukrainian speech
of their long-drawn-out whistles.

[23-27 December 1936]

148

14. 'A train of sledges'

The distant signs of a train of sledges
through the window of the sanatorium.
The river appears to be close
because of the warmth and the frost.
And what forest is that? A fir one?
It's not fir, but lilac!
And is that a birch there?
I can't say for sure –
just the prose of airy inks,
illegible, and light.

[26 December 1936]

15. 'This winter touches me'

This winter touches me
like a gift late in coming,
I love its wide reach
that develops out of uncertainty.

It is beautiful in its fear,
like the menace of threats.
Even the raven is afraid
before all the forest clearing.

The pale blue of the hemispherical, protuberant ice
of streams and sleepless lullabies
is unstable, but more
powerful than anything.

[29-30 December 1936]

16. 'The Cat'

All these misfortunes are because
I see before me
the magnifying eye of the cat.
It's the grandson of the stagnant weeds,
and the merchant of sea water.

There where Kashchei treats himself
on fiery cabbage soup,
it waits with the speaking stones
for who luck will bring as guests.
It touches the stones with its claws,
and nips the gold of nails.

In its sleeping quarters
a cat lives not to play –
its burning eyes contain
the treasure of the squinting mountain.
And in those icy pupils,
pleading, begging,
round sparks revel.

[29-30 December 1936]

17. 'Let it be blessed'

The reserve of weak,
sensitive eyelashes protects
your pupil in its heavenly rind,
as it looks into the distance and down.

Let it be blessed
and live long in its homeland –
cast the surprise pool
of your eye to catch me!

Already it looks willingly
at the ephemeral ages –
bright, rainbowed, fleshless,
still pleading.

[2 January 1937]

18. 'The Angry Lamb'

Smile, angry lamb, from Raphael's canvas,
the mouth of the universe, but it's different now...

In the light air of the pan-pipes the pain of pearls dissolves.
The salt has eaten into the blue, blue colour of the fringe of the ocean.

The colour of robbery is in the air, deep as a cave,
the folds of a stormy peace flow like cloth onto the knees.

The young reeds on the cliff are rougher than stale bread
and the entrancing power of the sky flows within the frame.

[9 January 1936]

19. 'The Sorcerer'

When the sorcerer brings out
the gossiping browns
and chestnuts
in the downcast branches,

the small but strong
bullfinch, the faded lazy hero
who's passing the winter
does not want to sing.

Under the vault of the eyebrows
of the overhanging sky,
I will quickly take my seat
on the lilac sledge.

[9 January 1937]

20. 'Like a ringed hawk'

I am held fast in Koltsov's ring
like a ringed hawk,
no one brings me messages,
and there are no steps up to my house.

The blue pine forest
is chained to my leg.
The view around is wide open,
like a messenger without orders.

The mounds of grass in the steppe are like nomads.
They're always on the move!
Night rests, nights, nights of little rest,
as though they were carrying the blind.

[9 January 1937]

21. 'Yeast of the world'

Dear yeast of the world –
sounds, tears and work –
rainy stresses
of trouble brewing,
and from what ore can one recover
the sound losses?

In the beggar memory
first you'll sense the blind ruts,
full of copper water –
and you'll follow in the tracks,
unknown, unloving yourself,
both the blind man and the guide.

[12-18 January 1937]

22. 'Little devil'

A little devil in wet fur crawled in –
well, where's he going? Where?
Into the thimbles made by hoofs,
into the hurried tracks:
robbing from the settlement
kopeck by kopeck the tribute air.

The road splashes in little mirrors.
The exhausted tracks
will remain a little longer
without covering, without sparkling mica.
The wheel grumbles, slants,
and then collapses: that's a minor disaster.

But I'm depressed – my direct
task gabbles perversely:
something else passed through it,
mocked me, and broke the axle.

[12-18 January 1937]

23. 'The Beggar Woman'

You're still not dead, you're not alone yet,
not while you revel with your friend the beggar woman
in the grandeur of the plains,
in the mist, the cold and the snowstorm.

Live, calm and comforted
in luxurious poverty, in powerful deprivation.
These nights and days are blessed,
and sweet-voiced work is without sin.

Unfortunate is the man who is scared by the shadow of himself
as by barking, and the scything wind,
and poor is he who begs alms from the shadow
and is himself half-alive.

[15-16 January 1937]

24. 'Into the face of the frost'

Alone, I look into the face of the frost,
it goes nowhere; I come from nowhere.
The breathing miracle of the plain
is always ironed out, flattened without wrinkles.

The sun squinting in starched poverty
is calm and comforted.
The decimalised forests are almost the same...
and the snow crunches in the eyes, as innocent as fresh bread.

[16 January 1936]

25. 'Oh, this slow asthmatic vastness'

Oh, this slow, asthmatic vastness –
I am sated with it to the point of refusal.
Give me a blindfold over my eyes,
when the horizon recovering its breath is wide open.

I would have got on better with the sand
lying in layers on the jagged banks of the Kama river,
I would have held on to her shy sleeve,
her eddies, banks and pits.

I would have learnt to work with her – for an age, or a moment –
jealous of the besieged rapids,
I would have listened to the fibrous age rings developing
under the bark of the logs in the current.

[16 January 1937]

26. 'The deadliness of the plains'

What can we do with the deadliness of the plains,
with the extended hunger of their miracle?
What we think of in them as openness
we behold as we fall asleep;
and the question is always growing: where are they going and
        coming from?
And isn't that man crawling along them slowly,
the one about whom we scream in our sleep:
the Judas of future nations?

[16 January 1937]

27. 'Don't make comparisons'

Don't make comparisons: the living are incomparable.
I had come to terms with the flatness of the plains
with a sort of fond fear.
The curve of the sky was a disease to me.

I would turn and wait for some service or news
from my servant the air.
I would get ready for a journey
and sail along the arcs of travels that never began.

I am prepared to wander where there is more sky for me,
but the clear anguish will not let me go
away from the youthful hills of Voronezh
to the civilised hills, that I see so clearly in Tuscany.

[18 January 1937]

28. 'Feminine silver burns'

How the feminine silver burns
that fought with oxidation and alloy!
Quiet work silvers
the iron plough and the voice of the poet.

[beginning of 1937]

156

29. 'Mount Elbrus'

Now I'm caught in a sunlit spider's web –
black-haired, and light brown.
The people need light, pale blue air,
and they need bread and the snow of Mount Elbrus.

There's no one to give me advice,
and I don't think I can work it out on my own.
There are no such transparent, crying stones
either in the Crimea or the Urals.

The people need a poem that is both mysterious and familiar
so that from it, they should wake up for eternity
and bathe themselves in the flaxen-curled,
chestnut wave of its sound.

[19 January 1937]

30. 'Meteorite'

As the meteorite from the heavens wakes the earth somewhere,
the exiled line fell to the ground, not knowing its father.
What is implacable is a godsend for the creator –
it couldn't be anything else; no one judges it.

[20 January 1937]

31. 'Human heads'

Heaped hills of human heads go off into the distance.
I grow smaller there, they won't notice me anymore;
but in much loved books and children's games,
I shall arise to say that the sun is shining.

[1936 – 1937]

32. 'The early ice'

I hear, I hear the early ice
rustling under the bridges,
I remember how the bright intoxication
flows overhead.

When Dante's lips were exhausted
he sang even more powerfully
from the squares with their palaces
and from the rough staircases,
about his circle in Florence.

So my shadow gnaws with its eyes
at that grainy granite,
and at night sees rows of logs
that in the daytime appear as houses.

Either the shadow twiddles its thumbs
and yawns with you,

or it makes a noise in public
warming itself with their wine and sky,

and feeds the importunate swans
with sour bread.

[21-22 January 1937]

33. 'I love the frosty breath'

I love the frosty breath,
and the confession of wintry steam.
Ah. I am I. Reality is reality.

The boy, the little lord of his sleigh,
the leader of the gang,
rushes past, red as a torch.

I am at odds with the world, with freedom –
I indulge in the infectiousness of the sleigh,
in its silver brackets, its tassels.

The age could fall lighter than a squirrel,
lighter than a squirrel to the soft stream.
Half of the sky is wearing winter boots.

[24 January 1937]

34. 'This January'

In this January where can I go?
The chasmed town is wildly obstinate.
Have the locked doors made me drunk?
I want to bellow because of all the bolts and locks.

The sidestreets are like snarling stockings,
and in the storerooms of the distorted streets
the hooligans hide quickly
in little corners and then run out.

I slide into the warty dark of the pit,
on my way up to the frozen over pump-house
where I trip and eat the dead air
as the rooks scatter feverishly.

And I let out a sigh and shout
at the frozen wooden tub:
'Oh for a reader, a counsellor, a doctor!
oh for a conversation on the barbed staircase!'

[1 February 1937]

35. 'Tragedies'

Where is the bound and nailed down grown?
Where is Prometheus, helping to support the cliff?
And where is the vulture, yellow-eyed and scowling,
its talons flying in pursuit?

The tragedies will not return. It will not happen.
Let these advancing lips
lead you right to the essence
of Aeschylus the stevedore, and Sophocles the lumberjack.

Prometheus is an echo and a greeting. He is a landmark, no –
            a ploughshare.
The open-air stone theatre of the growing times
has got onto its feet – and now everyone wants to see everyone:
those born, doomed and who have no death.

[19 January – 4 February 1937]

36. 'Like Rembrandt'

I have gone, like Rembrandt, martyr to light and shade,
deeply into this time which is growing ever-number.
There is a sharp pain in my burning rib
which is not protected by this soldier
nor by these guards who sleep under the storm.

Will you forgive me, great brother,
master, father of the black and green darkness?
The eye of the hawk's plume
and the hot coffers in the harem at midnight
cause only dire trouble
to a generation in uproar from the wineskins at twilight.

[4 February 1937]

160

37. 'The breaches of circular bays'

I had only just come to value the breaches of circular bays,
the pebbles and the blue of the sky, a slow sail
that merges into a cloud, and I am separated from all of you.
The seaweed, longer than an organ fugue,
is bitter, a pretence of hair and smells of the long lie.
My head is intoxicated with an iron tenderness,
and rust gnaws into the slightly sloping shore...
Why is a different sand laid under my head?
All my rights are here, in this flat region,
or in the throaty Urals, or in the broad-shouldered area around
　　　　the Volga,
and I must still breathe them in deeply.

[4 February 1937]

38. 'Wedding in the Caucasus'

I sing when my throat is moist, my soul dry,
my vision is humid enough and my conscience plays no tricks.
Is the wine healthy? Are the wineskins healthy?
Is the rocking in Colchis's blood healthy?
The chest constricts, is quiet, without language.
It is no longer I who sings. My breathing sings,
my hearing is sheathed in the mountains and my head is deaf.

An unselfish song is praise to itself,
a comfort to friends and tar to enemies.

The one-eyed song is growing out of moss,
a single-voiced gift of the hunter's life
which is sung on horseback and in the mountains.
They breathe freely and openly,
caring only about bringing the young ones
to the wedding in honesty and anger, without sin.

[8 February 1937]

39. 'Eyesight of Wasps'

Armed with the eyesight of slender wasps,
sucking at the earth's axis, the earth's axis,
I feel everything that ever happened to me,
and I memorise it, but it's all in vain.

I don't draw and I don't sing,
and I don't play the violin with a black-voiced bow.
I drive my sting only into life, and love
to envy the powerful, cunning wasps.

Oh, if I could be compelled
by the sting of the air and the summer warmth
to pass through the worlds of dreams and death,
to sense the earth's axis, the earth's axis...

[8 February 1937]

40. 'Eyes sharper than a honed scythe'

The eyes were sharper than a honed scythe –
a cuckoo and a drop of dew in each pupil.

They had scarcely learned at their full power
to distinguish the solitary multitude of stars.

[9 February 1937]

41. 'The worn grandeur of my soles'

He can still remember the wear and tear on his shoes,
and the worn grandeur of my soles.
I, in turn, remember him: his many voices,
his black hair, how close he lived to Mount David.

The pistachio-green houses on the fox-hole streets
have been renovated with whitewash or white of egg;
balconies incline, horseshoes shine, horse – balcony,
the little oaks, the plane trees, the slow elms.

The feminine chain of curly letters
is intoxicating for eyes enveloped in light.
The city is so excessive and goes off into the timbered forest
and into the young-looking, ageing summer.

[7-11 February 1937]

42. 'The words from the Kremlin'

Dream-sleep defends my hibernation on the Don river,
while armoured tortoises manoeuvre
swiftly and urgently, and the rugs
people unfold with their talk are fascinating.

Words I know well lead me into battle
for the defence of life, defence of my country, the earth,
where death will fall asleep like an owl in daytime.
The glass of Moscow burns between cut-glass ribs.

The words from the Kremlin are indefensible:
in them is the defence of defence,
and the armour of war; even though the brow and the head
together with the eyes are assembled amicably.

The earth listens, and other countries too, to the war-like chimes
that fall from the choir stalls:
the choir sings in time with the clock chimes:
'men and women slaves must not be slaves.'

[18 January – 11 February 1937]

43. 'On stations and piers'

The powerful milestone of the age
is looking from under the sweep of his eyebrows
at the noise and bustle of people
on stations and piers.

I found out, he found out, you found out.
Then go where you like,
into the chattering undergrowth of the station,
or to wait by the mighty river.

That stopping place, where darkness
clouded the eyes, is far away.
There was a tin mug on a chain
and a container of boiled water.

The Komi-Perm language was spoken,
passengers were fighting,
and the reproving stare of those eyes on the portrait on the wall
looked at me fondly – and drilled into me.

Many future deeds are still hidden
in our airmen and harvesters,
in our comrade rivers and thickets
and in our comrade towns.

I can't remember the past:
lips are hot, words are rough,
a white curtain flapped,
the rustle of iron foliage was carried in the air.

When we got going it was quiet,
only the steamboat sailed on the river.
The buckwheat flourished by the cedar,
a fish swam on the stream's conversation.

I entered the Kremlin without a pass,
to see him, to see his very heart.
As I burst the canvas of distance,
my head felt heavy with guilt.

[January 1937]

44. 'The engraver's soaring art'

As wood and copper were, for Favorsky, the engraver's soaring art,
we are neighbours with time in the boarded air.
We are all led by the layered fleet
of oak planks and sycamore copper.

The resin still seethes, oozing in the rings of the wood,
but is the heart only terrified flesh?
My heart is guilty and I am part of the core
of this hour that has expanded into infinity.

This hour feeding countless friends,
hour of menacing squares with happy eyes.
I shall look again at the whole area of the square,
all that square with its forests of banners.

[11 February 1937]

45. 'Buried in the lion's den'

I am buried in the lion's den and into this fortress
I sink lower, lower and lower,
listening to the yeasty cloudburst of sounds
stronger than the lion, more powerful than the Pentateuch.

How closely your voice calls me:
mankind before the commandments,
like the strings of ocean pearls,
and like the slender baskets of Tahitian girls.

The strong deep notes of your chastising song
are like an advancing continent.
The savage sweet faces of spoiled daughters
are not worth the matriarch's little finger.

My time is still limitless,
and I accompanied the joy of the universe,
like the quiet organ's playing
accompanies a woman's voice.

[12 February 1937]

THIRD
VORONEZH
NOTEBOOK

1. 'The sleepy, sleigh-tracked town'

The sleepy, sleigh-tracked town,
half-town, half-mounted-shore,
was harnessed to red coals,
warmed by the yellow mastic,
and overheated to burnt sugar,
and was carried away, on a crimson board,
to the cone of the steep hill,
extravagantly drunk on snow.
Don't search in it for the heaven of wintry oils,
of the Dutch skating school.
There are no merry gnomes, croaking and gnarled,
in hats with big ear flaps, flocking here.
Don't embarrass me with comparisons.
Cut off my drawing, which is in love with the firm road,
as the smoke running off on stilts
carries away the dry, but living maple leaf.

[6 March 1937]

2. 'If our enemies captured me'

If our enemies captured me,
and people stopped talking to me;
if they deprived me of everything in the world:
the right to breathe and open doors
and to assert that life will go on,
and that the people judge like a judge;
if they dared to hold me like a wild beast
and started to throw my food on the floor,
I would not keep quiet. I would not suppress the pain,
but describe what I am free to describe.
Having swung the naked bell of the walls,
and having woken the corner of the hostile darkness
I would harness ten bulls to my voice
and pass my hand through the darkness like a plough.

And in the depth of the watchful night
the eyes would flare at the labourer's earth.
Compressed in the legion of brothers' eyes,
I would fall with the weight of the whole harvest,
with all the compression of the oath rushing into the distance,
and the flaming years will swoop like a flock:
Lenin will rustle by like a ripe storm,
and on the earth, that avoids decay,
Stalin will destroy reason and life.

[first weeks of February to beginning of March 1937]

3. Rheims-Laon

I saw, in the segments of a rose window,
a lake, standing perpendicular,
in which fish played, building their home in the fresh water,
and a fox and a lion fought in a dug-out boat.

There were three baying portals out of which
diseases looked, enemies of the hidden arcs.
A gazelle ran across a violet expanse
and the cliff suddenly sighed under its towers.

The honest sandstone has risen, drunk with moisture,
from the midst of the cricket craftsmen's town,
the ocean boy bubbles out of a fresh stream
and throws cups of water at the clouds.

[4 March 1937]

4. 'France'

France, I ask for your land and honeysuckle
as I pray for pity and favour,

for the truths of your turtle-doves and the lies
of dwarf vineyards with their protective gauze.

In the light December your pruned air
becomes covered with hoar frost, minted, hurt.

To have a violet in prison, is to go mad and break the bounds.
A song whistles, carefree, mockingly,

where the crooked July street
seethed, washing away the kings.

But now in Paris, in Chartres, in Arles
good old Charlie Chaplin rules.

In an oceanic bowler hat he fidgets and swaggers around
with the flower girl, in confused preciseness.

There with a rose window on its breast, in a two-towered sweat
the shawl of the spider's web is turning to stone.
It's a pity that the roundabout's thanks are feather-light
and that it revolves and breathes in the town.

Godless woman, with the golden eyes
of a goat, bend your neck,
as you tease the beds of stingy roses,
rolling your r's with crooked secateurs.

[3 March 1937]

5. Rome

This is the city that loves to say yes to the powerful,
where frogs of the fountains, having croaked
and splashed about, sleep no more.
Awake, they cry with all the power
of their spouting throats and shells.
The city that loves to say yes to the powerful
is sprinkled with amphibian water!

There is a summer antiquity, light, naked,
with a greedy look, and flat feet as though it were
the undestroyed bridge of the Angel,
on the shallow steps above the yellow water...

The city is pale blue, modelled, ashy
in the drumming growth of houses.
The city sculpted with the swallow of a cupola
from side-streets and from draughts,
was turned by you into a nursery of murder.
You the hirelings of brown blood,
the Italian blackshirts,
you the evil whelps of dead Caesars.

                    *

Michelangelo, all your orphans
are clothed in stone and shame.
The statue 'Night' is damp from tears,
the young, fleet David is innocent.
Moses lying still on a bed
is like a waterfall.
The power of freedom and the lion's strength
are silent, sleeping and enslaved.

The ponderous Rome-man
languid as sea sponges
raised, in the square

where the stairs flow like rivers,
little terraces of furrowed staircases,
made, not for crippled and crippling sensual pleasures,
but so that footsteps might ring out like actions.

The Forum is excavated again,
and the gates are open for Herod.
The heavy chin of a degenerate dictator
hangs over Rome.

[16 March 1937]

6. Poem to the Unknown Soldier

1

Let this air and the thudding
of its long-range heart be a witness.
This air, which actively devours the trenches,
like oceanic, claustrophobic poison gas.

Even the stars are informers.
Why do they always need to look
into the oceanic, claustrophobic poison gas,
judging both judge and witness?

Rain, bleak sower
of the air's anonymous manna, remembers
how the forest of little crosses marked
the ocean of mud, the wedge of war.

The freezing, ill people
will kill, starve and be cold;
and the unknown soldier will be laid
to rest in his famous tomb.

Teach me, sickly swallow,
who has forgotten how to fly,
how I can keep control of this grave in the air,
without rudder or wing.

I will give a stern report
on Lermontov, Mikhail:
only the grave can straighten the hunchback,
and the chasm in the air is seductive.

2

These worlds threaten us
with rustling grapes,
with berries of poisonous cold.
These worlds hang like pillaged towns,
threatening us with golden slips of the tongue and informers.
The golden, expanding constellations dripping fat
are like vast awnings.

3

Through the atmosphere significant to the power of ten,
the light of velocities is ground into a beam,
the counting begins, and is made transparent
by the bright pain and the swarm of noughts.

Beyond the field of fields, flies
a new field like a wedge of cranes.
The news flies along a new path of light particles,
and yesterday's battle lights up the sky.

The news flies along a new path of light particles:
I am not Leipzig, I am not Waterloo,
I am not the Battle of the Nations, I will be the New –
clear bright light to the world.

4

Arabia is a mess, a bloodbath.
The light of velocities is ground into a beam
which stands on my retina
with its oblique soles.

Millions killed cheaply
have trodden out a path in the wilderness,
good night, all the best to them
on behalf of the earthwork fortresses.

The incorruptible sky over the trenches,
a sky of vast, wholesale deaths;
so integral, I follow you, flee you
and the words I mouth take flight in the darkness.

The gloomy, pock-marked
and humbled genius of the desecrated graves
is beyond the craters, the embankments and the scree,
over which he lingered sullenly.

5

The foot soldiers die well,
and the night choir sings well
over the flattened smile of Schweik,
the bird's spear of Don Quixote
and its chivalrous claw.
The cripple will be friends with man:
work will be found for all of them.
Along the outskirts of the age
a little family of wooden crutches clatters –
Comrades uniting the globe of the earth!

6

Is it for this that the skull must develop,
the entire forehead – temple to temple –
so that into its precious eye sockets
the troops could do nothing but flow in?
The skull develops through life,
the entire forehead – temple to temple –
teases itself with the cleanness of its seams,
enlightens with its dome of understanding;
foams with thought, dreams of itself –
the chalice of chalices, homeland of homelands;
the little cap sewn with starry ribbing –
the little cap of happiness – the father in Shakespeare.

7.

The clarity of the ash and the vigilance of the sycamore
overloaded and fainting,
rush home, tinged with red,
to colour both skies with their dull fire.

Only the superfluous is allied to us,
ahead is not failure but the testing.
To fight for the atmosphere we live on:
this achievement is not an example to others.

My conscience is overloaded,
my existence faint.
Is it I who am forced to drink this broth
and to cannibalise my own life under fire?

Is this package of enchantment
prepared in empty space,
so that the white stars should rush back home
tinged with red?

Night, stepmother of the stars' gipsy camp –
do you hear what will happen now and later?

8

Aortas are flooded with blood
as whispers run through the ranks:
'I was born in ninety-four,
I was born in ninety-two...'
Herded with the human herd
I squeeze my worn-out birth tag in my fist,
and whisper with bloodless lips:
'I was born in the night of the second
to the third of January in the irresponsible year
eighteen ninety-one – and
the centuries surround me with fire.'

[1-15 March 1937]

7. 'I will whisper this'

I will whisper this as if it were a rough draft,
because it's not time yet:
the play of the unaccountable sky
will be achieved by effort and experience.

Under the temporal sky
of purgatory we often forget
that the happy granary of the sky
is both an expanding and lifelong home.

[9 March 1937]

8. The Last Supper

The Last Supper sky fell in love with the wall –
it was hacked with the light of wounds and scars –
it collapsed into it, brightened,
turned into thirteen heads.

Here it is, my night sky,
before which I stand like a boy.
My back grows cold, my eyes ache,
I catch the firmament which is like a battering-ram.

And under each blow of the ram
the headless stars shower down:
the new wounds of the same fresco,
and the gloom of an unfinished eternity...

[9 March 1937]

9. 'Lost in the sky'

What can I do, lost as I am in the sky?
Let the one close to the sky answer.
It was easier for Dante's nine circles of hell
to ring out like athletes' discuses,
choking, turning black and blue.

You who are standing over me,
if you are the winebringer and cupbearer
then give me the strength without the empty froth
to drink to the health of the spinning tower,
to the hand to hand fighting of the crazy blue sky;
if I am not of yesterday and if I am not in vain.

Dovecotes, darknesses, starling boxes,
slender images of the bluest shadows,
vernal ice, divine ice, spring ice,
clouds are the warriors of charm:
Quiet! They're leading a storm cloud by the bridle.

[9-19 March 1937]

10. 'What can I do, lost as I am in the sky'

What can I do, lost as I am in the sky?
Let the one close to the sky answer.
It was easier for Dante's nine circles of hell
to ring out like athletes' discuses.

You can't separate me from life – it dreams
of killing and caressing at once,
so that the nostalgia of Florence fills
the ears, the eyes, the eye sockets.

Don't put on me, don't put
the bittersweet laurel on my temples,
it's better for you to tear my heart
into ringing blue bits.

And when I die having served my time,
the friend for life of all living people,
let the sky's response burst out
louder and higher in my cold breast.

[9-19 March 1937]

11. 'Perhaps this is the point of madness'

Perhaps this is the point of madness,
perhaps this is your conscience:
the knot of life in which we are recognised
and untied, so that we may exist.

The ray-spider in good conscience
lets out the cathedrals of crystals from another world
onto the ribs, gathering them again
into one integral beam.

The grateful beams of clear lines
directed by the silent ray,
will gather together sometime,
like honest guests,

and this will be here on earth, not in heaven,
as in a house filled with music.
Just take care not to frighten nor wound them.
It will be good if we live to see it.

Forgive me for what I say.
Quietly, quietly read it to me.

[15 March 1937]

12. 'Little Star'

Oh, how I wish
I could fly along a star beam,
unknown to anyone,
where I wouldn't exist at all.

And you, you must shine in a circle,
there is no other happiness,
and learn from a star
the meaning of light.

It is only a beam,
it is only light,
because it has the power of a whisper
and the warmth of murmured words.

And I want to say to you
that I am whispering,
that I entrust you, my child,
to the starbeam with this whisper.

[23 March – beginning of May 1937]

13. Winejug

You are the guilty debtor of a long thirst,
the wise procurer of wine and water,
on your sides, the young goats dance
and the fruits ripen to the music.

The flutes whistle, swear and are angry
at the trouble on your black and red rim
and no one can take you up
and put this trouble right.

[21 March 1937]

14. 'Joyful Crete'

Blue island, joyful Crete, famous for its potters,
whose talent has been baked
into the ringing earth. Do you hear
the subterranean beat of the dolphins' fins?

The sea is remembered
by clay made happy in firing.
The vessel's chill power
has cracked into sea and passion.

Give me back what is mine, Crete,
blue, soaring island, give me back my work,
and fill the fired vessel
from the breasts of the flowing goddess.

This was, turned blue, and was sung,
a very long time before Odysseus,
before food and drink
were called 'mine'.

Get well then, be radiant,
star of the ox-eyed heaven,
and you, flying fish of chance,
and you, water saying 'Yes'.

[21 March 1937]

15. 'My Nereids'

Nereids, my Nereids,
mourning is food and drink for you.
My sympathy is offensive
to the daughters of Mediterranean tragedy.

[March 1937]

16. 'Flutes'

The theta and iota of the Greek flute,
as though its fame were not enough for it,
unsculpted, unaccountable,
grew, suffered, bridged the gaps.

And it's impossible to leave it,
if you clench your teeth, you still cannot silence it,
and you cannot move it with your tongue into words,
nor mouth it with your lips.

The flautist will know no rest,
it seems to him that he's alone,
that at one time he moulded his native sea
out of lilac clays.

He hastens to be economical,
chooses sounds, crisp and spare
with a ringing, ambitious whisper,
with the patter of his lips remembering.

We cannot follow in his tracks,
the clods of clay are in the palms of the sea,
and when I became full of the sea,
my measure became the plague.

As for my own lips I don't like them;
murder is rooted in them.
I am forced to incline the equinox
of the flute to decline into nothing.

[7 April 1937]

17. 'The state shame'

The state shame of the Egyptians
was adorned with pedigree dogs –
the dead were endowed with all sorts of things
and the pyramid stuck up – a mere trifle.

He lived mischievously alongside the gothic,
and spat on the spider's rights,
the insolent schoolboy and robber angel,
the incomparable François Villon.

[18 March 1937]

18. 'Some wife searches'

Some wife, I don't know whose, searches
the streets of the monster Kiev for her husband.
And on her waxen cheeks
not one tear drop has streaked.

Gipsy girls don't tell fortunes for beauties.
The violins don't play in the Kupechesky park.
Horses have fallen in Kreschatik
and the aristocratic Lipki smells of death.

The Red Army soldiers have got
right out of town on the last tram.
And a soaked greatcoat cried out:
'We'll be back. Just you wait!...'

[April 1937]

19. 'The buds cling with a sticky promise'

The buds cling with a sticky promise,
look, a shooting star –
that's a mother saying to her daughter
not to hurry.

'Wait', half of the sky
whispered distinctly,
and a sloping rustle answered
'If only I had a son!'

I will begin to celebrate
a completely different life,
a cradle will rock
under a light foot.

The upright, wild husband
will be gentle and obey.
Without him, as in a black book,
it's frightening in the stifling world.

The summer lightning hesitated
at the comment and gave a wink.
The elder brother furrowed his brows:
the little sister complains.

The velvet heavy-winged wind
adds notes to the pipe:
let the boy have a strong forehead
and be like both of them.

The thunder will ask his friends:
'Did you ever hear
of a lime tree being given in marriage
before the cherries blossom?'

Bird cries come from the fresh solitude
of the forest –
the matchmaker birds whistle
their flattering homage to Natasha.

Such promises cling
to the lips, that, I tell you honestly:
eyes rush together to drown in
the thunder of horses' hoofs.

Everyone keeps rushing her:
'Bright Natasha,
get married for our happiness,
for our health.'

[2 May 1937]

20. 'I present the green promise'

I present the green promise
of sticky leaves to my lips –
taken from the faithless earth:
mother of snowdrops, maples and the little oaks.

Look how I become strong and blind,
submitting to the humble roots,
and isn't this thundering park
all too splendid to see?

The frogs, like globules of quicksilver,
have voices which couple them across the earth,
and the twigs become branches
and steam becomes a milky fantasy.

[30 April 1937]

21. 'The pear and the cherry blossom'

The pear and the cherry blossom aimed at me,
disintegrating as they beat me unerringly.

Clusters of blossoms in stars, stars in clusters of blossom –
what is this double power? Where does truth blossom?

It fires its flower into the air.
Its airy, white full blossoms flail it to death.

The sweetness of the double scent cannot be endured –
it fights and spreads, mingled, and fragmented.

[4 May 1937]

22. To Natasha Shtempel

I

Limping against her will over the deserted earth,
with uneven, sweet steps,
she walks just ahead
of her swift friend and her fiancé.
The restraining freedom
of her inspiring disability pulls her along,
but it seems that her walking is held back
by the clarity of a concept:
that this spring weather
is the ancestral mother of the grave's vault,
and that this is an eternal beginning.

II

There are women, who are so close to the moist earth;
their every step is loud mourning,
their calling is to accompany the resurrected,
and be first to greet the dead.
It is a crime to demand kisses from them,
and it is impossible to part from them.
Today angels, tomorrow worms in the graveyard,
and the day after, just an outline.
The steps you once took, you won't be able to take.
Flowers are immortal. Heaven is integral.
What will be is only a promise.

[4 May 1937]

NOTES

TEXTS

In 1973 the prestigious Biblioteka Poeta series had published a much-delayed volume of Mandelstam edited by N. Khardzhiev but it was very incomplete in the later poetry and, to add insult to injury, was introduced by a party hack, A. Dymshits. (For a full discussion of this introduction see Victoria Shweitzer's Russian article in *Keep my Speech*, published by the Mandelstam Society 1991.)

There has in the last years been a series of Mandelstam texts, published in Russia, including a Voronezh University Edition of *The New Poems*, as Mandelstam called *The Moscow Notebooks* and *The Voronezh Notebooks*, with articles and Nadezhda Mandelstam's Commentary to the poems, which comments also on the separate V. Schweitzer Ardis USA edition (1981), based on the Princeton archive of Mandelstam, of *The Voronezh Notebooks*. The culmination is a two-volume edition edited by P. Nerler, which draws on the work of Nadezhda Mandelstam and I. Semyonko and seems to be as near to perfect in its textual accuracy as we can expect. The first volume of this edition, published by Khudozhestvennaya Literatura, took over for us from the excellent Struve/Filipoff collection which was published in the West in 1967. For the dating of the Voronezh poems we have followed the Khudozhestvennaya Literatura text. For the order of the three notebooks we followed Nadezhda Yakovlevna Mandelstam's *Third Book* (YMCA Press), and Jennifer Baines' *Mandelstam: The Later Poetry* (Cambridge University Press), which draws heavily on Nadezhda Mandelstam's *Third Book* (Russian only as yet) although Jennifer Baines' book (now, very regrettably, out of print) was in fact published several years before *Third Book*.

The Mandelstam Society has published an authoritative chronological four volume edition of the Collected Works of Mandelstam. It should be mentioned that these volumes are almost devoid of commentary – the reader is referred to the Khudozhestvennaya Literatura edition with its fine commentary.

A new book has been published in Russian by the Mandelstam Society, Natasha Shtempel's *Mandelstam in Voronezh*. Natasha Shtempel, who limped on her left leg, was a young teacher who befriended the Mandelstams in Voronezh, when other people were afraid to approach them. She also kept an album of Mandelstam's poems, which survived the war – Voronezh was in the front line in 1942-43, and Natasha Shtempel was evacuated. She is the subject of several poems in the last part of the *Third Voronezh Notebook*, including the last poem of the book.

NOTES

1: This opening poem, which in its dating of 1934 is almost outside *The Voronezh Notebooks*, is probably addressed to Nadezhda Mandelstam, although Mandelstam did not show it to her in its entirety. Some Russian editors have attributed the dedication to Maria Petrovykh: 'the expert mistress of guilty glances/who has such slender shoulders' of the last poem in *The Moscow Notebooks*. However, the second verse about ironing seems to indicate Nadezhda Mandelstam. Mandelstam mentioned in a letter to his friend Livshits how well she ironed his shirts; and the tying of bundles or baskets recalls her from an earlier poem (*Moscow Notebooks* I.11: 'or find some bits of string/to tie up the bundle before dawn') There is a gap of well over a year before the next poem in the *First Voronezh Notebook*.

2: Mandelstam had written in 'The Word and Culture': 'Poetry is a plough, turning up time so that its deep layers, its black earth appear on top.' This poem is dedicated to Sergei Rudakov, who was in exile from Leningrad and whom the Mandelstams met in Voronezh. Rudakov was going to write, with Mandelstam, a full commentary on Mandelstam's poems. In Nadezhda Mandelstam's writings he appears to be a bit of a megalomaniac but they trusted him with many manuscripts, and indeed Akhmatova gave him her Gumilyov archive to work on. He left Voronezh for his home town Leningrad in July 1936, well before the end of the Mandelstams' exile in Voronezh, but in the Voronezh hospital, where he was being treated for scarlet fever, he had talked to Natasha Shtempel about the Mandelstams, and this was the reason (although he forbade her to see them) that Natasha was able to find and befriend them. He was killed in the war and most of the manuscripts and any commentary perished. Emma Gerstein has written a book *New Material on Mandelstam*, (in Russian: Atheneum, 1986), which draws on Rudakov's letters to his wife, and has a wealth of material on Mandelstam and his composition technique ('he pronounces four hundred lines for four').

'Black Earth': R.B.H. Watson writes: 'The Russian *chernozem* is a rich soil type characteristic of the temperate grasslands of the Russian steppe. The summer drought and winter frost favour the accumulation of humus provided by grass roots which die each year. During the dry season groundwater is drawn towards the surface and calcium carbonate is precipitated. Under the influence of the ascending calcareous solution the humus becomes black and insoluble. It stretches from the Carpathians and the Black Sea to the Urals and towards Siberia. "Chernozem" is also found in the prairies in the US.' There were particularly fertile fields of Black Earth belonging to the Agronomic Institute near where the Mandelstams lived.

'land and liberty': the congress of the populists 'Land and Liberty' was held in Voronezh in 1879.

3: Ivan the watchman was a hero of Russian folk song. He was hanged by the prince for his love for his wife the princess.

In chapter 30 ('The Disappointed Landlord') of *Hope Against Hope*, Nadezhda Mandelstam describes the flats and rooms in which they lived in Voronezh. The 'crotchety landlord', an agronomist who let them a room was disappointed: 'I thought you'd have writers like Kretova and Zadonski coming to see you, and we'd all be dancing the rhumba together.' Zadonski, and Kretova, who gave birth to the baby featured in 'Birth of the Smile', were members of the Voronezh Union of Writers. Later, at the end of his stay, Kretova was 'forced by circumstances' to accuse Mandelstam in an article of being a Trotskyist, *Kommuna* 23rd April 1937. 'The landlord' ('khozyain') was also a common name for Stalin.

5: See Krivulin Introduction. As Natasha Shtempel said, Mandelstam got neither the 'raven' (in its sense as the secret police van) nor the 'robber's knife' from Voronezh.

6: At midnight Radio Moscow plays the National Anthem and the chimes of the Spasskaya Tower clock on Red Square to which Mandelstam is listening with his earphones (the same word as for informers) on his crystal set. Emma Gerstein writes that Mandelstam used often to listen to music on the radio and was 'in love with the radio'. The first line of the Moscow metro was being completed at the time. The wine referred to in the original is 'Ai', a still champagne from the Epernay region in France. It is mentioned in Pushkin and in Baratynsky in the poem 'Feasts' (1821), which was written during his exile in Finland, where the wine is compared with a fervent mind not tolerating captivity. This section of the Baratynsky poem was censored, which his contemporary Zhukovsky complained about in a letter to Vyazemsky.

7: In the Russian the first line of this 'geography lesson' about Red Square would seem to have Stalin's Georgian name Dzhugashvili encrypted: Da ya lezhu v zemle gubami shevelya. This poem was left by Nadezhda Mandelstam in *The Voronezh Notebooks*, although in recent Russian editions it has been relegated to the back of the book, where there are six or seven poems that do not fit into *The Voronezh Notebooks*. The curve of Red Square on both axes is remarkable. The last line of the poem has an echo of Pushkin's late poem 'Exegi Monumentum'.

8: 'There was little of the straight line in him.' The Mandelstams lived for a time in their second of five flats that they had in Voronezh on 'Ulitsa Lineinaya' ('Straight Line Street') in a house in a hollow or virtual pit, now called Shveinikov Backstreet. The third line of the second stanza of the poem was originally: 'He lived on Lenin street', but Mandelstam did not include this line: the conflicting names would be even more dangerous. Nikita Struve, in his book in Russian *Osip Mandelstam: His Life and Times* (OPI, 1988) draws a parallel with Akhmatova, where in *Requiem* (which she was writing about this time) she proposes that if a statue to her is to be built it should be outside the 'Kresty' ('Crosses') prison in Leningrad (or rather St Petersburg, since it is still not there) where she waited in line with her prison parcel for her son, and where her first husband Nikolai Gumilyov was briefly incarcerated before being shot in 1921.

9: There is a macabre association with the children having their hair clipped for May Day and having their heads cut off, i.e. capital punishment ('the highest degree'). *The Voronezh Notebooks* were written down, mainly by Nadezhda Mandelstam, in purple ink (which according to Nikita Struve was the only colour ink available), and a V for what was known as the Vatican Codex was put after each of them and they were dated accurately. Some of the more dangerous poems were written down in a homemade code. This was the first poem Mandelstam composed after moving to the centre of the city. There was at this time the possibility of work in radio and in the theatre, – from 7th October 1935 to 1st August 1936, Mandelstam was a literary consultant with the Voronezh Theatre and wrote a programme on 'Goethe's Youth', and 'Gulliver' for children in 1935 for local radio.

10: Now "established" in Voronezh, Mandelstam felt able to look back in the next poems to the harrowing journey and time in Cherdyn. Mandelstam insisted that both of the first two poems should be included together as separate, albeit overlapping, poems for eventual publication – the second one being the censored version and the third a transition into 'Stanzas'. They describe the river journey up the river Kama into exile in Cherdyn (in the virgin forests of Perm) and back down on the trip to Moscow before going to Voronezh. According to Y.L. Freidin's useful article 'The Road to Voronezh' (*Mandelstam: Days in Voronezh*, Voronezh University, p.17): 'The forced journey to the Urals lasted less than a month, from 28th May 1934 to the end of June.'

11: For 'Stanzas', see Krivulin Introduction.

'Stanzas' was supposed to be a reconciliatory poem, and was one of the poems that Mandelstam tried unsuccessfully to get published.

III: 'I must live, breathing, growing big and Bolshevik.' Mandelstam mentioned to Nadezhda Mandelstam that one of the reasons the Bolsheviks were so successful lay in the root of their name being 'Bolshoi' ('big' or 'grand'). Mandelstam mentions the word 'Bolshevik' in two poems dated May 1935, which are outside *The Voronezh Notebooks*: 'The world began terrifying and great:/a black fern in a green night,/the Bolshevik is raised on layers of pain...'; and 'I am a non-party Bolshevik,/like all my friends, and like this enemy.'

IV: 'I jumped into my mind.' Mandelstam was admitted to Cherdyn Hospital. While there he suffered from paranoia that he was going to be shot. The jump – Nadezhda was left holding his jacket at the open window – was an unsuccessful suicide attempt from the high first floor window of the hospital, when he only injured his arm, landing in a flower bed, and as Mandelstam writes it was therapeutic. See 'The Leap' (Chapter 15, *Hope Abandoned*). In the same hospital he thought he was going to be taken and shot at six in the evening, but Nadezhda Mandelstam managed, without him noticing, to move the clock hands on round past the menacing hour and this seemed to calm him.

VII: 'working with speech, not listening to my inner ear, with my companion.' By 'not listening to my inner ear' Mandelstam would have been undermining the very basis of his method of composition, which was to mumble and mutter the lines of his poetry, to work from the spoken word, not to ignore it. The 'my companion' refers to Nadezhda Mandelstam. The gardener and the executioner is a reference to Hitler, who had at that time been in power for over a year. Lorelei sat on a rock combing her hair, luring the Rhine boatmen to their deaths.

VIII: *The Song of Igor*, a medieval Russian epic about Prince Igor's fight with the Polovtsians: 'Mandelstam could now, like the poet enchanter of the epic, lay his magic fingers on the taut, living strings and those strings would thunder glory of their own accord again as in the Song of Igor.' Jennifer Baines, *Mandelstam: The Later Poetry* (p.130).

12: The journey from Moscow to Sverdlovsk or Solikamsk most probably took five days (a five-headed monster as Jennifer Baines describes it) by train for the five of them, the Mandelstams, accompanied by three guards of the GPU (forerunner of the KGB), and then a further boat journey on to Cherdyn as described in I.10. Os'ka, the senior guard, read aloud Pushkin's 'Gypsies', which Nadezhda had brought along with them. In his essay 'The Slump' (*Russia* No. 3, 1924), Mandelstam had written: 'The distortion of a poetic work in the reader's perception is an inevitable social phenomenon. It is difficult and useless to fight it: it is easier to spread electrification throughout Russia than to teach all literate readers to read Pushkin as he is written, rather than as their spiritual needs require or their intellectual capacities allow' (translated by Constance Link from *Osip Mandelstam: The Collected Critical Prose and Letters*, p.204). The last stanza and the next poem refer to the Vasiliev brothers' film *Chapayev* of 1934, which Mandelstam had seen in Voronezh while Nadezhda Mandelstam was on a visit to Moscow in April 1935. 'For almost the first time in the history of the Soviet cinema the film showed the White army not as cowards and bandits but as opponents and heroic ones. The film ends with the death of the commander of the Red partisan brigade, Vasily Chapayev, who drowns in a river, felled by a bullet.' (Notes: G. Struve and B. Filipoff, Mandelstam Inter-Language Literary Associates, 1967.)

13: 'In the Vasilievs' sound film *Chapayev* one of the most powerful episodes is the "psychological attack" of the White officers on the cavalry of Chapayev. The officers advance on the cavalry and machine-gunners in a tight foot formation, with Russian cigarettes clenched between their teeth, not paying attention to the machine-gun fire which mows down their ranks. Others rise into the places of those who have fallen, and the tight formation of officers moves on with threatening force against the partisan cavalry. "The admiral's cheeks were scraped/ with the English horse razor": this refers to the episode of the shaving of the colonel of the Whites, one of the heroes of the film, and the "admiral's cheeks" of the

Supreme Commander Kolchak.' (Notes: G. Struve and B. Filipoff Mandelstam Edition.)

14: Compare Ovid (the poet *par excellence* of exile), *Tristia*, Book 3, Elegy 7: 'Everything that it is possible to take has been taken from me, / only my gift is inseparable from me, and I am comforted by it: / in this matter Caesar has no rights over me.'
Walking was an integral part of Mandelstam's composition technique. In the Russian *'stopa'* means both a 'foot' and a 'metrical foot'. Mandelstam had studied Classics at the Tenishev Lycée in St Petersburg. For Mandelstam creation came from the movement of the lips, and the voice; see I.7.

15: This poem was written while Nadezhda Mandelstam was on a trip to Moscow, on hearing of the death in 1932 of Olga Vaksel in Oslo (his informant told him it was in Stockholm, and did not mention it was suicide), with whom Mandelstam had been briefly and stormily in love in the winter of 1925, and 'who had been his wife's only serious rival for his affections during his married life' (Jennifer Baines, p.134). Her great-grandfather was the composer-violinist A.F. Lvov, composer of the Russian National Anthem. The last stanza is full of references to Goethe: Mandelstam was writing a version of 'Goethe's Youth' for the local radio, where Mignon is mentioned: 'The shy little girl with the harp is Mignon. She is a Southern girl, but not Italian, who has lost her homeland; she is the embodiment of longing for the flourishing South.' There are also references to Schubert and his song cycles 'The Beautiful Miller Maid' (*Die Schöne Müllerin*) and 'Winter Road' (*Die Winterreise*), also to be found in the next poem. According to Keith Owen Tribble, 'It is important to note also that these Schubert songs were once performed by Olga Vaksel' (*Mandelstam Days in Voronezh*, Voronezh University, 1994, p.82).

16: This poem is dedicated to Olga Vaksel.

17: This poem is connected with Mandelstam's radio play *Goethe's Youth*.

18: Marina Mnishek (1588-1614), Polish Princess, wife of the false Dmitry (see Pushkin's *Boris Godunov*). Marina Tsvetayeva identified herself with her. The violinist is Galina Barinova, who played a concert, instrumental for Mandelstam's return to poetry, at Voronezh on 5th April 1935, and who reminded Mandelstam of Tsvetayeva. The three devils in the last stanza, according to Nadezhda Mandelstam, are Marina Tsvetayeva, Olga Vaksel and herself, but

B.A. Kats in his brilliant short book in Russian on Mandelstam and music, *Osip Mandelstam: 'Full of Music, the Muse and Torment'* (Leningrad, 1991), indicates that the three devils may be Paganini, Mephistopheles (from the poem 'Faust' of Lenau), and either Satan, or the devil with the violin in Stravinsky's 'Soldier's Story'. Voronezh was one of the few provincial towns that had a symphony orchestra and many musicians were invited to play there. Mandelstam attended concerts and even rehearsals, and wrote programme notes.

19: Sergei Rudakov describes this poem as being 'about the sea and old Istanbul', whereas Nadezhda Mandelstam claims it is about the Five-Year Plans which could not be written about directly.

20: In June 1935, after one of her visits to Moscow, Nadezhda Mandelstam brought back to Voronezh not only the news and rumours surrounding the murder of Kirov, which was to precipitate the full-blown Stalinist terror, but also the pebbles and semiprecious stones they had gathered in Koktebel on the Black Sea. There is an untranslatable pun in the word 'opal', the precious stone and 'opala', 'exile'. Mandelstam chooses the simple soldier of the deep sea: a grey pebble. See Nadezhda Mandelstam, *Hope Abandoned* (Collins Harvill, pp.471-72).

21: The dedication is to V. Kuibyshev whose test pilot son was killed in a plane crash. 'The Airmen', which could have become the start of a cycle, is a first approach to 'The Poem to the Unknown Soldier'.

22: The editors of the recent Russian editions have put this poem in *The Moscow Notebooks* near the Wolf Cycle, because it was written on the back of 'The Wolf' manuscript, despite Nadezhda Yakovlevna's cogent argument that according to its context and content (ripped gauze and carbolic referring perhaps to the charred airmen's bodies) it comes at the end of the *First Voronezh Notebook*.

In his childhood Mandelstam used to go to a dacha in Terioki in Finland. 'Life "flared up" suddenly for him through a chance remark by one of his numerous governesses who, on listening to his childish efforts at literary composition, declared that 'there was indeed something there' – one of the high points of his childhood' (Jennifer Baines, p.142). See Nadezhda Mandelstam, *Hope Abandoned*, p.473-79.

SECOND VORONEZH NOTEBOOK

1: Sadko was a minstrel-merchant famous in the epic songs of old Russia. 'Sadko, too accomplished musically for his own good, had delivered himself into the clutches of the "king of the sea" in exactly the same way as Mandelstam's disgrace at the hands of his own 'tsar' had come about – through too effective a use of his art' (Jennifer Baines, p.147).

We have used 'whistle' where some would use 'hoot' or 'hooter'. Mandelstam said to Nadezhda: 'Perhaps I am that whistle.' By a strange cross-cultural coincidence the American poet William Carlos Williams in his 1935 collection in the title poem 'An Early Martyr' has: 'Let him be/ a factory whistle/ That keeps blaring –/ Sense, sense, sense!'

2: The baby son with the smile was the writer Olga Kretova's. Jennifer Baines (p.148) points to the cognition theme of Mandelstam's 'Octets' (*The Moscow Notebooks*, II. 21): 'The tiny attribute of sixth sense,/ the eye in the crown of the lizard,/ the monasteries of snails and shells,/ the flickering little conversation of antennae...', and says 'Circles and arcs, such as characterise a snail's shell or the eye of a primitive animal form, appear in both [poems]. In "Octets" the curves of rainbows and billowing sails, of cupolas and arc-like bends enhance the sense of roundness: "and space, drawing green forms/ with the sweeping arcs of racing sailing boats"; "and suddenly, out of my mumblings/ sounds fill out and stretch" and "like a road, which bends into the shape of a horn,/ trying to grasp the abundance of inner space/ and the pledge of the petal and the dome." An identical series of images – rainbows, back-bones, mountain ridges – echoes in "Birth of the Smile".' The curved lips of the poet, mouthing the words of the poem, are equated with the baby's lips that smile before they speak.

'Titanic moment': literally 'moment of Atlases' – Atlas was the Titan who held the world upon his shoulders. Not much further light is shed on this obscure word, which has elsewhere been mistranslated as Atlantis, by the fact that 'Atlases' are also the name for male caryatids, especially the ones that are at a back entrance of the Hermitage Museum.

4: In the many variants to these two poems about the goldfinch, there is a couplet: 'I react to my likeness:/ to live like a goldfinch is my decree.' Mandelstam gave a goldfinch to Vadik, the son of their landlady. 'The little boys nearby set traps and ran a bird market': Nadezhda Mandelstam, *Third Book*.

6: Mandelstam said that Alexander Blok would have envied him this poem, which is a hark back to warships coming into the harbour in Petersburg. Blok has a similar poem: 'Do you remember how the green water/ slept in our sleepy bay/ when the warships entered/ in line ahead' (vol.3, p.136 of 8 vol. Collection, Moscow, Leningrad 1960-1963).

8: Nadezhda Mandelstam asked who 'they' were. 'Were they the people?' But Mandelstam replied that was too simple. 'Mandelstam explained the abundance of "theirs" in this poem as a result of the influence of Spanish phonetics. He was reading *El Cid* at the time and the Spanish poets. But his version of Spanish phonetics was probably a fantasy' (Nadezhda Mandelstam, *Third Book*).

9: At one stage Mandelstam declared this poem was to the Assyriologist Shileyko, Akhmatova's second husband. This was when the idol's smile was 'quietest', rather than 'broad', and the poem included the variant line 'he begins to live when guests arrive'. Later, as he completed the poem, Mandelstam realised the poem was to Stalin and this reading is supported in a Russian article by Mikhail Meilakh (*Life and Art of Osip Mandelstam*, Voronezh University, 1990). The poem is about the Titan Atlas – turned into a mountain as a punishment for his fight with the gods – but Meilakh also mentions the Georgian Prometheus myth of Amirani, who was shackled to Mount Elbrus in the Caucasus, and later in the article quotes from the 'Ode to Stalin': 'I want to thank the hills,/ that they developed his bone and wrist:/ he was born in the mountains and knew the bitterness of prison./ I want to call him not Stalin, but Dzhugashvili.' In 'mountains', '*gorakh*', and 'bitterness', '*gorech*', is contained the birthplace of Stalin: 'Gori'. We took the decision not to include our version of the 'Ode to Stalin' (not to be confused with the fateful epigram to Stalin in *The Moscow Notebooks*, II. 20, 'We are alive but no longer feel'), thus respecting, we believe, the Mandelstams' wishes. Of the 'Ode to Stalin', written between January and February 1937, in a vain attempt to save their skins, Mandelstam said to Akhmatova: 'Now I realise it was an illness'. The powerful poem II. 31 which comes from the 'Ode' shows that it was far from purely laudatory and this section alone would be reason enough for Editors in the Russia of the late 30s not to print it. 'The final variant was completed in March 1937 and it was sent to some Moscow publishing houses. Later, Mandelstam demanded that the text of "The Ode" be destroyed,' observes Pavel Nerler in the Khudozhestvennaya Literatura Edition, where interested Russian readers can nevertheless read it. It is also to be found in the fourth volume of the Struve Filipoff collection, and in English translation in *A Coat of Many Colours* (Berkeley, CA) by Grigory Freidin. During the writing of the 'Ode to Stalin' (for this poem Mandelstam did indeed write at table with pencil and paper, 'like any other writer' as Nadezhda Mandelstam puts it) many fine anti-ode poems arose. This was examined in a groundbreaking article by Clarence Brown: 'Into the Heart of Darkness', *Slavic Review*, XXVI (1967), p.584-604.

11: The pine wood was on a hill in front of their dacha in Zadonsk which the Mandelstams had rented the previous summer. See Note to II. 21.

12: Before writing this poem, Mandelstam spread Nadezhda's watercolours of Zadonsk on the floor. Nadezhda Mandelstam had trained as an artist.

13: The snow was very late in coming that winter and the fields around were soaked with rain. In the first section of this poem Mandelstam describes the plywood illuminated map (shaped like Africa) at the telegraph station very close to their house. Vorobyovko was the regional centre village from which Mandelstam's tour of the collective farms had started in the summer of 1935, when he had been commissioned to write poems in praise of them. These poems did not come about, no more than a book about the Voronezh area that Mandelstam was hoping to get an advance to write, or another book that Mandelstam was going to write on the Urals 'on the old route'. However S.V. Vasilenko and Y.L. Freidin have published in the third volume of the Mandelstam Society Collected Works fifteen pages of unfinished 'Drafts for a Documentary Book' about Nikolskoye village in the Vorobyovo region.

14: From 18th December 1935 to 5th January 1936, Mandelstam was in a 'nerve' sanatorium in Tambov for treatment of his heart disease. He says in a letter to Nadezhda Mandelstam (3rd January 1936) that his stay in the sanatorium 'brought on a depression', and he also mentions his desire for his exile to be transferred to the Crimea.

15: Written after the first latecoming snow had fallen in Voronezh.

16: Kashchei was an evil sorcerer in Pushkin's *Ruslan and Ludmila* and many other fairy tales. In a letter dated 31 December 1936 to N.S. Tikhonov, Mandelstam says: 'In this poem I have made a real piece of gold with very modest means and the help of the letter "shch"... The Russian language is capable of miracles if only the line is humble before it, learns from it and fights with it boldly... This poem of mine will some day be printed along with others, and it will belong to the people of the Soviet lands, to whom I am infinitely indebted.'

17: This poem is to the Mandelstams' domestic cat. Originally Nadezhda wanted to put it after 'The Angry Lamb' since the contrast between Kashchei's cat and their own seemed too abrupt.

18: 'Nadezhda Mandelstam is not sure to which painting the poem about the angry lamb refers. While the obvious choice is Raphael's *Madonna Conestabile*, hanging in the Hermitage, she thinks that in certain undefinable ways it bears a greater resemblance to Leonardo's *Madonna Litta*, which Mandelstam would also have seen there. Since they had no reproduction of either, the poem represents a general longing for the riches of the Hermitage' (Jennifer Baines, p.172). On the other hand G. Struve and B. Filipoff say in their notes: 'It is very possible that Mandelstam has in mind the *Madonna Alba*, which was in the Hermitage but was sold to America around 1936 (to the Mellon Collection *c.* 1937). The sale of the best pictures in the Hermitage by the Soviet government in 1935-37 was reckoned then by the Russian intelligentsia to be a national disgrace and a national disaster. Perhaps this is why the poem has "smile *angry* lamb". (The lamb is the Christ child); he is angry that "robbery is in the air", although after its sale it is touched by "the mouth of the universe", the picture is "different now". We don't in any way insist that this is the meaning of the poem: but perhaps it was the direct cause for its being written.'

19: 'I will quickly take my seat/ on the lilac sledge' refers to the sledge of the dead. See Akhmatova's epigraph taken from Vladimir Monomakh's 'Sermon to his Children' for 'The Way of All the Earth': 'He sat on the sledge and set off on/ the way of all the earth.'

20: A.V. Koltsov (whose name contains the word: 'koltso' – 'ring') was a nineteenth-century folk poet who lived in the Voronezh area.

21: Nadezhda Mandelstam wrote: 'In the summer of 1936, thanks to money given us by Akhmatova, Pasternak and my brother, Evgeny, we were able to get out of Voronezh and spend some time in the country. This was very important because of M.'s heart trouble, which was getting worse and worse. We decided to go to

Zadonsk, on the upper reaches of the River Don, once famous for its monastery and the monk Tikhon... For six weeks we rested... but then we heard over the radio about the beginning of the terror... After listening to this, we walked out silently along the monastery road. There was nothing to talk about – everything was clear. That same day M. stuck his walking-stick into the imprints left by horses' hoofs on the roadway – it had been raining the day before and they were full of water. "Like memory," he said. These imprints turned up (as "thimbles made by hoofs") in verse written in the following January' (*Hope Abandoned*, Chapter 42, p.195). 'At the time when this poem was written, he had already begun to write the "Ode", which he hoped would save his life' (*Third Book*, p.236).

23: Mandelstam powerfully uses the word 'shadow' in his letters, now translated in *Osip Mandelstam: The Collected Critical Prose and Letters* (translated by Jane Gary Harris and Constance Link, Collins Harvill) One to Yury Tynyanov on 21st January 1937 reads: 'Please don't regard me as a shadow. I am still casting off my shadow.' Also in a letter to K.I. Chukovsky of 17th April 1937: 'I am a shadow. I do not exist. I have only the right to die. My wife and I are being driven to suicide.'

26: 'The Judas of future nations' (a variant has 'The Judas of unfounded space'): 'The historical perspective which caused Mandelstam to see him [Stalin] as the Judas not so much of present but of future generations was seldom achieved by his contemporaries in 1937, at the height of the Terror. No one could visualise the day when an objective history would assign to Stalin the role of the arch-traitor to humanity, for their own safety from his treachery occupied all their attention. Like Mandelstam, they saw him crawling out of every corner' (Jennifer Baines, p.181).

27: There is a very typical play on words in the third verse, where the word 'toska', 'anguish', evokes the word 'Tuscany'. Mandelstam had travelled to Italy as a young man; and for him Tuscany and Florence were the birthplace of Dante, who, with Petrarch, was his favourite Italian poet. Perhaps the resigned or conciliatory quality of this poem is because 'the Ode, such as it was, had been completed' (Jennifer Baines, p.182).

29: Mount Elbrus is the highest mountain in the Caucasus to which, in ancient myth, the Amirani/Prometheus figure was shackled.

31: Heaped hills: Mandelstam said to Nadezhda: 'Why when I think of him [Stalin] do I see before me heads, heaped hills of heads?' This quatrain is extracted from the 'Ode to Stalin'. See Note to II. 9.

33: Nadezhda Mandelstam: 'We were living on a hill, from which there was a steep descent to the river. The traces of this landscape are in many of the poems of this winter. The boys, among them Vadik, the son of our landlady, went down this steep slope to the river on their sledges. Round about this time the snow had fallen, which was late that year. O.M. said that from this poem it would not be difficult to guess that he had asthma in the frost: "Ah, I am I. Reality is reality." "Ya eto ya. Yav' eto yav" ' (*Third Book*, p.240). In a letter inviting his mother-in-law V.Ya. Khazina to stay [beginning of 1937], Mandelstam writes: 'As soon as Nadya goes away I am stricken with an agonizing psychosomatic illness which has the following symptoms: in recent years I've developed an asthmatic condition. *Breathing is always difficult.* When I'm with Nadya I breathe normally, but when she has to leave I literally begin to suffocate. Subjectively speaking, it is unendurable. I sense the end. Each minute seems like an eternity. When I'm alone I can't take a single step by myself' (*Collected Critical Prose and Letters*, Collins Harvill, p.559).

35: The Prometheus myth, foreshadowed by II. 9. comes into its own. Nadezhda Mandelstam does not know why Aeschylus is the stevedore and Sophocles the lumberjack, but thinks this may be a reference (not yet traced) to Annensky, the poet and translator of the Greek tragedies, or the work of the symbolist poet Vyacheslav Ivanov, at whose 'Tower' Mandelstam cut his poet's teeth as a young man.

36: The picture 'Procession to Golgotha' was in the Voronezh Museum and was attributed to Rembrandt, but according to the P. Nerler commentary it was in fact by a student of his, Jacobs Willems de Vetu the Elder.

37: The longing for the Crimea – Russia's entry onto the Mediterranean – never left Mandelstam, and he made documented efforts to get his exile transferred to there.

38: 'Is the wine healthy?' P. Nerler notes in his commentary to the Khudozhestvennaya Literatura edition: 'In the opinion of S. Lakoba this is a reference to the death of Nestor Lakoba on 27th December 1936 by poisoned wine in the home of L.P. Beria in Tbilisi. (Mandelstam had met N. Lakoba in 1930, who had told him of his distant ancestor who had been poisoned at a feast in the family home of his blood enemy.)'

39: The phonetic kernel of this poem in Russian is 'os', as it is for the 'Ode to Stalin'. 'Os' is axis, (or axle) 'osy' are wasps, 'sosut' is sip or suck, and 'os' is the same element in Osip Mandelstam – and Iosif Stalin. A bolder translation might play with cusp (for axis) and wasps, and sip, and Osip.

41: Mount David (Mtatsminda) is the mountain above Tbilisi in Georgia. The 'worn grandeur of my soles' is an echo of 'Conversation about Dante', where Mandelstam talks about how many pairs of sandals Dante must have worn through on the goat paths of Italy while composing *The Divine Comedy*. This is a comment on Mandelstam's method of composition while walking.

44: The engraver Favorsky did engraving illustrations for *The Song of Igor* as well as doing engravings at the funeral of Bely (see end of Mandelstam's *Second Moscow Notebook*). Mandelstam is wondering about whether he'll be present at the May Day celebrations in Red Square.

45: Nadezhda Mandelstam: 'A poem about the woman singer with the deep voice – and at the same time of liberation from "The Ode". O.M. listened to Marian Anderson [the black American contralto, who sang spirituals, often on Old Testament themes, and Bach, accompanied by the organ – Tr.], who was doing performances at that time in Moscow. He also saw her portrait somewhere. But there's not just Marian Anderson in this poem. Those days we found out that the woman singer from Leningrad, who had worked on the radio [Mandelstam translated the Neapolitan Songs for her – Tr.], had fallen ill. Someone whispered to us that she was not ill, but that her husband, an engineer, had been arrested. He had already spent quite a time in the camps. We visited her and found out the details of the arrest. She was hoping that her husband would not go back to the camps again and that he would be exiled and that she would go with him and they would be able to survive on her singing' (*Third Book*, p.244).

1: Nadezhda Mandelstam: 'This landscape poem was written, so to speak, from nature: it is the view of Voronezh from the river bank round about where Natasha (Shtempel) lived' (*Third Book*).

2: 'Stalin will destroy reason and life'. Nadezhda Mandelstam suggested to Mandelstam 'rouse'/'*budit*', instead of 'destroy'/'*gubit*', because it was impossible to send the poem with its last two lines in its proper form. Recent Russian editions (except for the tiny format complete poems edited by Y.L. Freidin, published in Perm) retain 'rouse', but it seems to me indisputable that Mandelstam could not *write* 'gubit'/'destroy', especially as he sent the poem to Korney Chukovsky. The fact that the variant 'rouse' is in all the copies should not rule out the reading 'destroy', although it has been argued that the ending does not fit the poem.

3: Mandelstam had visited France in 1910 as a young man. The poem completes the architectural cycle started in his first book *Stone*.

4: This is not only a nostalgic poem to France, but also, in the last stanza, an appeal to Maya Kudasheva, Mrs Romain Rolland, who was with her husband in Russia at the time. Mandelstam wanted her to intervene in his case with Stalin, 'a hope he cherished even in Vtoraya Rechka [the transit camp on the way to Vladivostok where it is most likely that he died – Tr.] after his arrest and imprisonment – but this time it was Rolland himself who was to be approached' (Jennifer Baines, p.205). Maya Kudasheva had trouble with her Russian 'rs', see Mindlin's 'Memoirs of Mandelstam in Theodosia' in the Struve/Filipoff edition, II, p.525. The Chaplin film referred to is *City Lights*, and Mandelstam was to write a poem to Chaplin not included in the *Voronezh Notebooks*.

5: The Rome of the Caesars and blackshirts is contrasted with its architecture and statuary. In the final verse there is a reference in the dictator monster to Mussolini. The 'Night', 'David' and 'Moses' are all sculptures by Michelangelo. 'David' however is in Florence, and 'Moses' does not lie but sits (as Mandelstam remembered but did not correct), and the fountains with frogs are in Milan rather than in Rome.

6. **Poem to the Unknown Soldier:** The modern critic, Vyacheslav Vs. Ivanov has some interesting things to say in his article ' "Poem to the Unknown Soldier" in the context of world literature', in

the Voronezh University Press Mandelstam edition: 'The theme of the poem is the destruction of millions during battle, when the skies threaten the land forces. The threat is described by means of many references to the speed of light: that is one of the basic leit-motifs of this part of the poem:

> Through the atmosphere significant to the power of ten,
> the light of velocities is ground into a beam.

and

> The news flies along a new path of light particles

Mandelstam himself, according to the rough drafts, was inclined to think that the whole "Poem to the Unknown Soldier" and especially the part connected with the mention of the speed of light was prophetic:

> This is the vision of the prophet,
> trampling with his soles the path in the wilderness.

...In the anti-war part of the "Poem to the Unknown Soldier" Mandelstam continues directly the pathos of a large part of the late works of Khlebnikov.'

6.1: In the third line of the poem (which went through very many variant stages) there was a variant mentioning the 'poison gas of Verdun', and our translation of these opening lines has born that in mind. Stanza 5 is an obvious reflection of Lermontov: 'In the ocean of the sky/ without rudder or sail/ the graceful chorus of heavenly bodies/ quietly floats in the mist.'

6.6: 'the father in Shakespeare'. O. Ronen in his useful Russian essay, 'On the subject of "The Poem to the Unknown Soldier" ' in *Word and Fate: Osip Mandelstam*, as well as pointing out that Flammarion's *Récits de l'infini: Lumen, histoire d'une âme*; *Histoire d'une comète*; *La vie universelle et eternelle* may be a subtext to the poem, also indicates, without giving the context, a passage in Joyce's *Ulysses*, which Mandelstam read in translation: 'When Rutlandbaconsouthamptonshakespeare or another poet of the same name in the comedy of errors wrote Hamlet he was not the father of his own son merely but, being no more than a son, he was and felt himself the father of all his race, the father of his own grand-father, the father of his unborn grandson who, by the same token, never was born...Himself his own father...Wait. I am big with child. I have an unborn child in my brain. Pallas Athena! A play! The play's the thing! Let me parturiate!' (Bodley Head edition, p.196, tracked down by my friend James Christie):

6.7: The receding stars are tinged red (or bloodied as O. Ronen puts it) by the Doppler effect.

6.8: The dates of birth in the poem would indicate that these are not conscripts, but people being consigned to the camps.

L.F. Katsis in his Russian article in *Word and Fate: Osip Mandelstam*, 'Byron and Mandelstam', tries to make a case for Byron's 'The Last Judgment' being a subtext to 'Poem to the Unknown Soldier'. The Byron poem was first published in Russian translation in 1904.

Mikhail Meilakh in his paper in Russian, 'About one Exotic Subtext in the "Poem to the Unknown Soldier"', in the *Mandelstam Centenary Conference Papers* (Hermitage, 1994), draws parallels with Gurdjieff's thinking, and offers the intriguing possibility of Mandelstam having met Gurdjieff, either just before the First World War at the Stray Dog cabaret in Petersburg or when Mandelstam visited Tiflis in 1920. Meilakh goes into detail on Mandelstam's 'Astrophobia' (an exception to which is 'Little Star', III. 12). He quotes part 2 as being particularly Gurdjieffian. Nadezhda Mandelstam records in *Third Book* (p.247) that 'Mandelstam remembered that Gumilyov had said that every poet has a special relationship to stars, and he [Mandelstam] complained that with him stars appeared when the material was ending.'

In the early 1920s Mandelstam had translated from the German a book of Max Bartel's (1893-1975) poetry. 'To the Unknown Soldier' and 'Verdun' Nos 127 and 137 in Volume 2 of the Mandelstam Society *Complete Works of O. Mandelstam* seem particularly relevant to the 'Poem to the Unknown Soldier'.

Nadezhda Mandelstam discusses the poem in *Hope Abandoned*, Ch. 35, 'Verse on the Unknown Soldier', p.483, where she indicates its oratorio qualities.

8: The poem refers to 'The Last Supper' fresco by Leonardo da Vinci in the Church of Santa Maria delle Grazie in Milan, which was severely damaged in the 17th and 18th centuries and in 1943 (Khudozhestvennaya Literatura, Notes). In the last verse 'the ram' in Russian is 'tarana', and 'tirana' – a vowel change away – means tyrant.

10: Jennifer Baines: 'Finding a solution to this dilemma [being lost in the sky – Tr.] presented a difficulty which Mandelstam compares with that of making the nine circles of Dante's hell resonate and ring out like an athlete's discus. He sees two alternatives ahead: the distasteful life of the *victor ludorum*, crowned with laurels – "the bittersweet laurel", or the disintegration of his body, to merge with the blue sky in a disembodied sound, a fate he finds preferable here...' (p.217).

12: Coming so soon after 'Poem to the Unknown Soldier' with its threatening stars, this intimate poem to Nadezhda Mandelstam about the little star redresses the balance. In many of his letters to Nadezhda, Mandelstam calls himself her nanny. But this is one of the only poems to Nadezhda in which that tender tone is applied.

13: Mandelstam frequently visited the Museum at Voronezh, which had a good selection of antique Greek pots. 'The wine jug in question belonged to the black-on-red type (late sixth century BC)... The Voronezh example, one of many such, depicted satyrs playing *auloi* – flutes – in an apparent fury... at the chipped or broken state of the rim of the pot' (Jennifer Baines, p.222).

14: In the first line we use the variant 'joyful', not 'green', which is the now established reading, but which conflicts with the blue island. The subterranean dolphins presumably refer to the dolphin friezes found in Crete by archaeologists. Mandelstam reconstructed this poem in Samatikha in spring 1938, but could not remember the two extra verses which were in the manuscript given to Rudakov in Leningrad at the beginning of 1938.

15: 'The fifty Nereids ("the wet ones"), who attended on the sea-goddess Thetis, were both beautiful and benevolent... the tears shed by miserable mortals, were as essential as their food and drink to these ocean dwellers...' (Jennifer Baines, p.224).

There are some poems missing in this section, of which Nadezhda Mandelstam only remembered fragmentary lines. One is about composers: Rameau, Tchaikovsky, Mozart; one is about the young Mycenaean lions and a relief from Saqqara; one about the Étoile in Paris; and one has a line 'There is a cabin for me on this ship' which coincides with the line in Akhmatova's poem 'Death':

I

I was on the brink of something,
to which I cannot hang a name.
This half-sleep calling,
this slipping away from myself.

II

I am already standing at the border of something
which comes to everyone at a different price.

208

There is a cabin for me on this ship,
and wind in the sails: the terrible moment
of parting with my own country.

[Dyurmen, 1942]

from *Anna Akhmatova: Selected Poems*, translated by Richard Mc-
Kane (Bloodaxe Books), p.156.

16: The composers in the missing poems lead on to 'Flutes'. The
lips (*guby*, the root 'gub' is also that of 'destruction') unite the
poet and the flautist. According to Y.L. Freidin, there was a pic-
ture in the Voronezh museum of a flautist, with Greek writing.
This poem was written on the arrest, for espionage, of Shwab, a
German flautist who was living in Voronezh, and played in the
orchestra. He used to play Bach and Schubert to Mandelstam.
Mandelstam wondered whether he had dared or been able to take
his precious flute to the camp. See *Hope Against Hope*, pp.186-87.

17: Nadezhda Mandelstam (*Third Book*) considered that this poem
should be made up of two quatrains, as opposed to the six quat-
rains as printed in the Nerler/Averintsev Khudozhestvennaya
Literatura edition. The last quatrain of the long version concern-
ing Villon reads:

He is the robber of the heavenly clergy,
it's no shame to sit by his side:
and before the very end of the world
the skylarks will ring out.

18: Kiev was the home town of Nadezhda Mandelstam. It 'takes
on the horrendous aspect of Gogol's supernatural monster, the
form in which it had revealed itself in 1919, during the year in
which the Mandelstams had met there' (Jennifer Baines, p.229).
'One day just before we left, when they were shooting hostages,
we looked out of the window... and saw a cart piled with naked
corpses. Some matting had been carelessly thrown on top of them,
but limbs were sticking out in all directions' (*Hope Abandoned*, p.20).

19: Natasha Shtempel, to whom this poem is addressed, was the
young school teacher due to be married, who brought joy into the
Mandelstams' lives. She visited them frequently and they went to
see her at her mother's. On the eve of their departure from
Voronezh, Mandelstam composed one of several quatrains to her:

Natasha's come back. Where has she been?
Don't worry, she hasn't eaten or drunk...
Black as night her mother can tell:
her daughter smells of wine and onion.

20: Written after a walk with Natasha Shtempel in the Botanical Gardens. 'It was deserted, no one was around. There was only the joyful croaking of frogs in the lakes, and the spring sky, and the trees almost without leaves, and the slightly green hillocks' (Natasha Shtempel, p.40).

21: Nadezhda Mandelstam said to Natasha Shtempel: 'This is about you and me.'

22: When Mandelstam gave this poem to Natasha Shtempel, he said: 'I wrote this poem yesterday. It is a love lyric. It is the best that I have written. When I die, bequeath it to Pushkin House.' Nadezhda Mandelstam writes in *Hope Abandoned*: 'The beautiful poems to Natasha Shtempel have a place all to themselves in Mandelstam's love lyrics. He always linked love with the thought of death, but in his verse to Natasha there is also a serene and lofty sense of future life' (p.248).

For insights into the life and work of Mandelstam, we are grateful to the following editors and scholars: Jennifer Baines, Sir Dimitri Obolensky, Victor Krivulin, Pavel Nerler and S. Averintsev, I.M. Semyonko, Gleb Struve and Boris Filipoff, Emma Gerstein, Mikhail Meilakh, Vyacheslav Vs. Ivanov, Natasha Shtempel, Nikita Struve, Clarence Brown, B.A. Kats, Alla Gelich; and for his gift of a small format *Complete Poems* published in Perm, made at the 1991 London conference on Mandelstam at SSEES, we owe thanks to Y.L. Friedin. Finally, Nadezhda Mandelstam's three books remain invaluable, and form the best commentary.

For other translations of the Voronezh poems, we recommend the following volumes by our fellow translators which, with the exception of *Stone*, contain relevant work: *Osip Mandelstam: Selected Poems*, translated by Clarence Brown and W.S. Merwin (Penguin Books); *Osip Mandelstam: Selected Poems*, translated by James Greene (Penguin Books); *Osip Mandelstam: Selected Poems*, translated by David McDuff (Writers and Readers; reprinted by Anvil Press); *Poems from Mandelstam*, translated by R.H. Morrison (Associated University Presses); *Osip Mandelstam: 50 Poems*, translated by Bernard Meares (Persea); *Osip Mandelstam: A Necklace of Bees: Selected Poems*, translated by Maria Enzensberger (Menard/Kings); and Osip Mandelstam's first book *Stone*, translated by Robert Tracy (Collins Harvill).

Recently Anvil Press has brought out the 1921-1925 poems of Mandelstam in my translation with commentary by Michael Basker in *Ten Russian Poets: Surviving the 20th Century*, a further step towards a complete Mandelstam poems in English which we are preparing.

Bereft of the possibility of translating Mandelstam from Russian (which is in itself a key international area of Mandelstam scholarship), especially since the 80s, Russian scholarship on Mandelstam has, so to speak, mushroomed. The Mandelstam Society in Moscow led by Pavel Nerler has been in the vanguard, with four collections of essays in Russian: *Keep My Speech*, including in 3/2 Joseph Brodsky's brilliant remarks at the London Mandelstam Conference in July 1991. *Osip and Nadezhda Mandelstam by their Contemporaries*, edited by O.S. and M.V. Figurnov (Natalis, Moscow), in Russian, contains fascinating transcriptions of the archive recordings of Duvakin. Also of interest are Emma Gerstein's *Moscow Memoirs*, translated by John Crowfoot (Harvill Press, 2003).

ENVOI

Nadezhda Mandelstam's last letter to Osip Mandelstam

22 OCTOBER 1938

Osia, my beloved, faraway sweetheart!
I have no words, my darling, to write this letter that you may never read, perhaps. I am writing it into empty space. Perhaps you will come back and not find me here. Then this will be all you have left to remember me by.

Osia, what a joy it was living together like children – all our squabbles and arguments, the games we played, and our love. Now I do not even look at the sky. If I see a cloud, who can I show it to?

Remember the way we brought back provisions to make our poor feasts in all the places where we pitched our tent like nomads? Remember the good taste of bread when we got it by a miracle and ate it together? And our last winter in Voronezh. Our happy poverty, and the poetry you wrote. I remember the time we were coming back once from the baths, when we bought some eggs or sausage, and a cart went by loaded with hay. It was still cold and I was freezing in my short jacket (but nothing like what we must suffer now: I know how cold you are). That day comes back to me now. I understand so clearly, and ache from the pain of it, that those winter days with all their troubles were the greatest and last happiness to be granted us in life.

My every thought is about you. My every tear and every smile is for you. I bless every day and every hour of our bitter life together, my sweetheart, my companion, my blind guide in life.

Like two blind puppies we were, nuzzling each other and feeling so good together. And how fevered your poor head was, and how madly we frittered away the days of our life. What joy it was, and how we always knew what joy it was.

Life can last so long. How hard and long for each of us to die alone. Can this fate be for us who are so inseparable? Puppies and children, did we deserve this? Did you deserve this, my angel? Everything goes on as before. I know nothing. Yet I know everything – each day and hour of your life are plain and clear to me as in a delirium.

You came to me every night in my sleep, and I kept asking what had happened, but you did not reply.

In my last dream I was buying food for you in a filthy hotel restaurant. The people with me were total strangers. When I had bought it, I realised I did not know where to take it, because I do not know where you are.

When I woke up, I said to Shura: 'Osia is dead.' I do not know whether you are still alive, but from the time of that dream, I have lost track of you. I do not know where you are. Will you hear me? Do you know how much I love you? I could never tell you how much I love you. I cannot tell you even now. I speak only to you, only to you. You are with me always, and I who was such a wild and angry one and never learned to weep simple tears – now I weep and weep and weep.

It's me: Nadia. Where are you?

Farewell.

Nadia.

[from *Hope Abandoned*, translated by Max Hayward]